The Winning Hand Workbook

Positive Youth Development
In 6 easy lessons

A PYD workbook for
Youth Workers, Mentors, and Teachers

JT (Jerry) Fest

DEDICATION

"Youth Worker" is not a title reserved for a specific job or career. It is a title bestowed on anyone who spends some or most of their time actively helping young people to navigate the world, pursue healthy growth and development, and/or defend their rights and achieve their dreams. Youth Workers take many forms; teacher, counselor, probation officer, mentor, parent, family friend, or dozens of other professions and relationships that help young people make the transition to adulthood.

Whether you are engaged with youth professionally or simply taking an interest in a young person who desperately needs someone to be on their side, you are a Youth Worker.

This workbook is dedicated to you, with much respect and gratitude.

CONTENTS

How to use this book   i

Lesson 1   1
An Introduction to the PYD Approach

Lesson 2   11
Youth Outcomes: The "Bottom Line" of Youth Work

Lesson 3   26
(s)OS: A Framework for Youth Development

Lesson 4   38
High Expectations

Lesson 5   52
Meaningful Participation

Lesson 6   64
Caring, Supportive Relationships

Appendices

   A - Bonus Lesson: Measuring Developmental Outcomes   81

   B - Youth Outcomes Chart   103

   C - Red Flags -- A Self-assessment for Youth Workers   104

   D - Spectrum of Youth Participation -- An Evolutionary View   108

   E - Guidelines for Attentive Listening and Reflection   109

   F - Principles of Win/Win Negotiation for PYD Youth Work   110

Footnotes   113

About the Author   117

How to use this book

For over 15 years, *Youth Development: A Winning Hand* has been offered as a live presentation throughout the United States and Canada. Considered one of the best introductions to the Positive Youth Development approach for new staff and practitioners wishing to see better outcomes for young people, *The Winning Hand Workbook* now makes the knowledge and skills taught through the live presentation available on demand in a concise, easy to use format.

The most important thing to understand about this workbook is that there is a greater emphasis on *work* rather than *book*. You cannot expect to derive the full benefits of learning simply by reading the content. *The Winning Hand Workbook* is designed to be a course of action, not a "lecture on paper." Throughout the workbook there are various instructions and assignments that are intended to be completed *in order and before* reading further. At the same time, completing the assignments provides you with a "learning journal" to which you can refer as you develop your skills with and practice of the Positive Youth Development approach.

The Winning Hand Workbook is divided into 6 primary lessons, along with a "bonus lesson" and additional resource materials in the appendices. Instructions are contained in the text of the workbook, so start at the beginning of Lesson 1 and work your way through the book at your own pace as directed, paying attention to the "stop" and "go" prompts as they appear. For best learning, *take your time*. Be sure that you are familiar with the content of each lesson before moving on to the next.

NOTE: While anyone can use this workbook on their own to improve their practice, many people will be using this as an "initial training" within a program, agency, or school. As such, it is designed to be used with supervisory support. Instructions are given in the text for a "supervisor substitute" if you are using this on your own. If you are a supervisor who will be working with staff using this workbook, it is highly recommended that you complete the course yourself before supervising its use by others.

Most of all, thank you for the work that you do. The field of youth work is both challenging and often unrecognized … but those in the field will tell you that it is also rewarding and *fun*. If that's not how you're finding it, you're doing it wrong. *The Winning Hand Workbook* will help.

Lesson 1
An Introduction to the Positive Youth Development Approach

The starting point is the belief that every youth has innate resilience.
~ Bonnie Benard ~

In this lesson you will learn:

- The Origins of the Positive Youth Development Approach (Resiliency Research)
- Protective Factors that Foster Resiliency
- Concept and Practice: Youth Development Definitions

The Origins of the Youth Development Approach (Resiliency Research)

The Youth Development approach (also known as, and used interchangeably in this workbook as, Positive Youth Development, or PYD) can trace its origins to decades of research into human resiliency which can be defined as an individual's capacity to face, overcome, and even be strengthened by adversity[1]. Human resiliency is our innate ability to form adaptive coping strategies in response to change and stress. This capacity for human resiliency is part of our "hard wiring" as human beings. Much as we are all born with an innate will to survive, we are also born with an innate capacity for resiliency.

Most researchers cite the *Kauai Longitudinal Research Study*[2] conducted by Emmy E. Werner and Ruth S. Smith as the starting point for a body of international studies on extremely high-risk children, tracking 698 children born on the island of Kauai in 1955 from birth to 40 years of age. Additional researchers, including Bonnie Benard and a host of others, built upon this study and postulated that all human beings have an innate capacity for resiliency, and it is the human capacity for resiliency that is responsible for the ability of significant numbers of high-risk children in various studies to overcome their challenges and develop into healthy and accomplished adults.

But *significant numbers* of children demonstrating resilient behaviors means that there is also a group of children that does not. Researchers were forced to ask; *why do some young people demonstrate resilient behavior, while others don't?* Their conclusion was that while all young people have an innate capacity for resiliency, external (environmental) factors can act to either *foster* or *inhibit* an individual's capacity. An analogy would be that all (healthy) children have the ability to run, but the environment in which they are running (sand or snow versus road or track) has a direct impact on their ability.

Most of us are familiar with the term Risk Factors[3], which refers to issues and challenges that young people face. When present, Risk Factors act like sand or snow on a runner, *inhibiting* a young person's innate capacity for resilient behavior, and rendering them less capable of healthy development.

But there are other environmental factors that can *foster* a young person's innate resiliency, and these are called *Protective Factors*. Protective Factors act like road or track on a runner, promoting healthy development and enabling young people to form adaptive coping strategies that help them to deal with and rise above the effects of Risk Factors in their lives.

Protective Factors that Foster Resiliency[4]

Protective Factors are discussed and defined differently in different sources, but the similarities are greater than the differences. While different numbers of Protective Factors may be described, most sources present the following three Protective Factors as the primary resiliency fostering conditions:

- High Expectations
- Meaningful Participation
- Caring and Supportive Relationships

High Expectations

Perhaps the most misunderstood Protective Factor; it may be easier to begin with an understanding of what this is *not*. High Expectations is not Positive Thinking. Positive Thinking is a form of optimism and, while an optimistic outlook can be an invaluable support for High Expectations, Positive Thinking alone is not what is meant by this Protective Factor.

Neither is High Expectations goals, measurements, or benchmarks. It is not creating hoops for young people to jump through or setting standards for young people to achieve. Goals, measurements, and benchmarks have their place, but they are not what is meant by High Expectations in the PYD sense of the term.

High Expectations are *the beliefs that young people experience about themselves* in response to the *people and environments around them*. Or, more accurately, it is a specific *quality* of these beliefs that serves to foster a young person's resiliency. Young people receive messages about what type of person they are and what they are capable of becoming through their experience of other's beliefs, words, actions, practices, and the environments that are created. If the messages are that a young person is good, competent, and capable, those messages will serve as a Protective Factor that will foster resiliency -- even if the young person doesn't yet believe it about themselves and is not currently acting that way.

Young people have an external locus of identity, that is, they tend to see themselves as they perceive that others see them. This is because they are still growing and developing and have not yet formed a solid self-image and "owned" their identity. As such, the beliefs and expectations that we have about young people will have a direct impact on their thoughts and behavior, serving as a Protective *or* a Risk Factor, depending on whether the expectations are *high* or *low*. In an environment of low expectations a young person is likely to have their innate capacity for resiliency *inhibited*. But in an environment of High Expectations, their innate capacity for resiliency can be *fostered*.

One of the things that make High Expectations challenging is that you can't *pretend* to have High Expectations of young people. You actually have to believe in their positive qualities, intentions, and potential. It is what you actually *believe* about young people that will come across in your words, tone, and actions, and this is where a young person will perceive your "expectations." Remember, most communication (estimated at between 60 and 90 percent) is non-verbal, and much non-verbal communication is reflective of our true beliefs and feelings. If you believe that young people are liars and manipulators, it's unlikely that you will be able to *pretend* that you believe differently.

Note that we are also talking about *environmental* messages. Look around your own environment and imagine that you are a young person. What would you know about *yourself* from the layout, the signage, the reading material, the furniture, the cleanliness (or lack thereof)? Everything the young person *perceives* communicates, so make sure that it sends the message that you *wish* to communicate.

High Expectations will be explored in greater detail in Lesson 4.

Meaningful Participation

This is sometimes referred to as "opportunities for" participation, but the relevant question is; participation in what? The answer can best be summed up as; anything that directly affects the individual young person, including but not limited to choices, decisions, actions, and environments. When an individual is a meaningful participant in matters that impact their life, that participation serves to foster resiliency.

But participation as a Protective Factor has a qualifier; *Meaningful*. When we speak of Meaningful Participation, we are saying that the participation must be *legitimate*. This goes beyond asking for youth input when you already know what you're going to do, or when the decision makers have little interest in or connection to what the young person thinks. It does *not* mean giving the young person all of the power and letting them do anything they want, but it *does* mean that the young person's participation is *real* and *valued*.

Meaningful Participation will be explored in greater detail in Lesson 5.

Caring, Supportive Relationships

Like expectations, relationships may foster *or* inhibit resiliency. Relationships that are abusive or exploitative become Risk Factors that *inhibit* resiliency. The qualifiers *caring* and *supportive* indicate specific *qualities* of a relationship that make it a Protective Factor.

Caring indicates that, *from the young person's perspective*, the relationship is based on genuine interest. This interest is not focused on who they may become, or what they have to offer, or what problems/deficits they are exhibiting. It is a genuine interest in who they are, *as* they are. It is knowledge that someone cares that you exist, for no other reason than that you are you ... not that you are part of a target population, or for the role that you serve, or for the benefits that you offer ... but simply because you are *you*.

Supportive indicates that, *from the young person's perspective*, the relationship is seen as a viable resource. It does not necessarily mean providing for them, but it does mean that they trust to access the relationship if needed. Maybe the relationship can't even do anything about a young person's situation, but they know it will be there if they need it.

As the number of caring, supportive relationships in a young person's life increases, so does the young person's capacity for resiliency. This is not to say that a single relationship of this type has little value; actually, a single relationship can be a great Protective Factor in a young person's life. But the more exposure one has to these types of relationships, the more resilient they will be.

Two additional qualities impact a relationship's value as a Protective Factor.

1. Both parties must have the same definition of the relationship. If you see yourself as the young person's counselor, but they see you as a friend, the relationship may *inhibit* rather than *foster* resiliency. Mutual clarity is a critical component of a fostering relationship.

2. Boundaries need to be appropriate to the nature of the relationship. Boundaries between two friends are not the same as boundaries between a counselor and client. Your boundaries need to be congruent with the type of relationship that you have established.

A final relationship consideration is that long term is generally more "protective" than short term. However, even a relationship of *a few minutes* can have deep and long lasting effects.

Caring and Supportive Relationships will be explored in greater detail in Lesson 5.

Concept and Practice: Youth Development Definitions

The Youth Development approach is sometimes referred to simply as Youth Development. However, "Youth Development" actually refers to a concept that *underpins* the Youth Development approach.

The *concept* of Youth Development is that we are all in a constant process of development where we are seeking ways to meet our basic physical and social needs, and build the competencies we need to be successful in our lives. We are actually referring to *human* development, but Youth Development theory states that this process is more pronounced when we are young. As we age, we learn what works for us and what doesn't, so our "seeking and building" tends to slow down and become more focused. As young people, we "seek and build" in a rapid, constantly changing, non-linear fashion.

This concept explains *all* behavior by young people, particularly the behavior that is sometimes difficult to understand. Why does a young person leave home to survive on the streets? Because they are seeking ways to meet basic physical and social needs, and build competencies. Why does a young person join a gang? Because they are seeking ways to meet basic physical and social needs, and build competencies.

Certainly, from most of our perspectives, based on our knowledge and experience, a decision to survive on the streets or join a gang is a very poor way to "seek and build." The key to understanding the decision is to realize that it is not made with *our* perspective, knowledge and experience, and that from the perspective, knowledge, and experience of the *decision-maker*, it may appear to be the most viable alternative.

The *practice* of Youth Development (the Youth Development approach, Positive Youth Development, or PYD) is a way of supporting the Youth Development conceptual process. It is an approach to working with young people that fosters their innate capacity for resiliency and supports their development. It is recognition that they are seeking ways to meet basic physical and social needs and build competencies, and it is working *with* them to present means to that end in a manner that is viable from their perspective.

The practice of Youth Development is a *way* of working with young people. It is an *approach*, not a model. It is not *what* you do, but rather it is the *way* that you do it. As a result, PYD is applicable to education, corrections, social services, parenting, or any program model that interacts with young people. The approach is the *environment*, not the structure, and the environment is focused on fostering young people's innate capacity for resiliency and supporting their development.

The Youth Development approach is simply a way of working with young people that makes their development the *focus* of our attention and the *measurement* of our success. This differs from most traditional "problem-based" approaches, where young people are identified as having some deficit, delinquency, or other "issue" that needs to be corrected. Instead, Youth Development assumes that *all* young people have the same developmental needs, *regardless* of any problems that they may or may not be facing, and believes that satisfying those needs will result in a healthy, accomplished, and fully functioning person.

Is PYD "Strength-based?"

Youth Development and "Strength-based" approaches are compatible and share many similarities, and as such they are often confused and/or represented as being essentially the same thing. However, there is an important distinction between these two approaches. A Strength-based approach begins with the identification of a problem, and then seeks to apply the person's innate strengths and capacities to the goal of surmounting that problem. For example, if I have a drug problem, a Strength-based approach will help me identify the resources I possess that will help me stop using drugs. By contrast, a Youth Development approach identifies only that I am a young person with developmental needs. Whether or not I am experiencing problems is only a description of the reality and environment in which I live. "Problems" I may be experiencing are not the focus of the Youth Development approach, nor is overcoming them the measurement of Youth Development's success. Just as all tomatoes are fruits, but not all fruits are tomatoes, all Youth Development approaches are Strength-based, but not all Strength-based approaches are Youth Development.

Summation

- There is a large body of research showing that all people have an innate capacity for resiliency, which means that we are all innately capable of facing, overcoming, and even being strengthened by adversity.
- Research also shows that external factors affect an individual's capacity for resiliency. Risk Factors *inhibit* resiliency. Protective Factors *foster* resiliency.
- Protective Factors are High Expectations, Meaningful Participation, and Caring and Supportive Relationships. These will each be explored later in greater detail in Lesson's 4, 5, and 6.
- This base of research became the foundation for a practice, or way of working with young people, that is known as the Youth Development approach, or Positive Youth Development, or PYD.
- Youth Development as a concept refers to a developmental *process* where young people seek ways to meet basic physical and social needs, and build competencies.
- Youth Development as a practice refers to an *approach* to working with young people that fosters their innate resiliency and supports their developmental process.
- Youth Development differs from Strength-based approaches in that it is developmental as opposed to problem focused.

STOP **Learning Assignment 1**
Complete **BEFORE** proceeding

NOTE: Several learning assignments in this workbook request that you interview one or more young people. You may either seek out different young people each time, or you may ask a few young people to serve as your learning partners throughout this course and seek their feedback with each assignment. It is not recommended that you offer *incentives* to your learning partners. If the incentive of assisting in your professional development is not sufficient, they probably won't make the best learning partner. However, you may offer *supports* (meeting over lunch and picking up the check; providing transportation, etc.). Think in terms of making it possible for them to assist you, as opposed to rewarding them for doing so.

Part 1: Interview one or more young people (19 or younger) and ask them the questions on the next page. Write or paraphrase their answers in this workbook so that you have a record of their thoughts. Be sure to define your terms and rephrase these questions as needed to ensure clarity. You may wish to use a conversational approach rather than simply asking the three questions. The process you use is less important than understanding the young person's perspective. Interviewing more than one young person is recommended. Remember, you are not trying to question or challenge the young person's perspectives, nor is it necessary that you agree with what they are saying. You are simply trying to hear them and understand.

Questions for Learning Assignment 1, Part 1

1. What do/can adults do that makes you feel capable, confident, or competent?

_____

_____

_____

2. Do you feel that adults generally include you and allow you to participate in decisions and choices? Why do you or don't you feel this way?

_____

_____

_____

3. What specifically do/can adults do that would make you feel cared about or supported?

_____

_____

_____

Part 2: <u>After</u> completing Part 1, meet with your supervisor* and discuss the following questions. Write the key points of your discussion below:

1. What did you learn from Lesson 1 and/or your interview(s) that was new for you?

_____

_____

_____

2. What did you re-learn or remember as a result of Lesson 1 and/or your interview(s)?

_____

_____

_____

3. List the key thoughts, points, or ideas that you want to remember from Lesson 1 and/or your interview(s). You may list as many items as you wish, but list at least 3.

_____

_____

_____

***NOTE**: If you do not have a supervisor, identify an adult who will be willing to serve as your learning partner. Use that person as your "supervisor." The goal is simply to have someone with whom you can discuss these ideas out loud.

Part 3: In preparation for **Lesson 2 - Youth Outcomes: The "Bottom Line" of Youth Work**, purchase or acquire a deck of poker-size playing cards. A poker-size deck can be found for as little as $0.50 in many stores. If any store wants more than $3.00, look elsewhere. Lesson 2 will explain the purpose of this deck.

 If you have completed Parts 1, 2, and 3 of Learning Assignment 1, you may now move on to Lesson 2.

Lesson 2
Youth Outcomes: The "Bottom Line" of Youth Work

We worry about what a child will be tomorrow,
yet we forget that he is someone today.

~ Stacia Tauscher ~

In this lesson you will learn:

- "Winning Hand" Lesson Anchors
- Lesson Anchor: The Ace of Hearts
- Achievement and Prevention Outcomes
- Developmental Outcomes
- Challenges to Developmental Outcomes

"Winning Hand" Lesson Anchors

The "Winning Hand" presentation has been designed around a concept called *anchoring*. This is a presentation technique that links learning to objects as a memory aid. Playing cards have been selected as the anchors for Youth Development concepts, thus the "Winning Hand" reference.

Throughout these lessons you will be asked to consider five different playing cards. If you have not yet purchased/acquired a deck of poker-size playing cards, **please do so before proceeding**. You will be asked to pull a card from the deck when it is referenced. As each card is referenced, place it in a location where you will see it often (e.g., your desk, your appointment book).

Lesson Anchor: The Ace of Hearts

The first card in your Winning Hand is the **Ace of Hearts**. Please draw it now and place it in a location where you will see it often. This is the anchor card for **Lesson 2 -- Youth Outcomes: the "Bottom Line" of Youth Work**.

Regardless of the *model* of youth work in which you are engaged, the outcomes that result are the most important aspect of your work. The Ace was selected to represent that outcomes are the primary focus of all youth work, but why the Ace of *Hearts*?

Hearts represent something that I believe about you, even though we have probably never met and may never meet. I believe this about you because you work with young people. Your profession may be teacher, counselor, administrator, social worker, therapist, outreach worker, juvenile corrections worker, substance abuse professional, residential advocate, or one of dozens of other occupations within the youth work field … it doesn't matter. Simply because you are in the field of youth work, I know something about you: You care about … have a *heart* for … young people.

How do I know this? Because I am familiar with the field of youth work. You are not in your job because of the generous pay and excellent benefits, nor are you there for the recognition you receive, or the lack of stress in the job. The only reason why a rational person would enter the youth work field is because they care about young people and want to see them succeed.

Because I know that you care about young people, I also know that you can think of at least one young person that you know or have known who holds a special place in your heart. It may be someone with whom you have worked, or a young person in your neighborhood, or your own child. For many of you, more than one young person comes to mind, but I want you to focus on just one *specific* young person. Think of their name, picture their face. Now, write them a letter …

Follow the instructions below. Do **NOT** read any further until you have completed this assignment.

Instructions: You have been asked to think of one specific young person you know or have known who holds a special place in your heart. Now imagine that you are present on the day of their birth. Maybe you were, maybe you weren't -- maybe they are much older now -- in any case, imagine that you are able to go back in time and be present when they are born. You have the opportunity to write them a letter that they will read later in life. What will you say? Use the form on the next page to create your letter. ***Do not skip this exercise***. You will use the letter later in this lesson.

On This Day of Your Birth

Date: _____

Dear Little _____

Welcome to the world!

I hope that you grow up to be (1) _____

_____.

I want you to experience (2) _____

_____.

and to always (3) _____

_____.

I know that you will learn to (4) _____

_____.

and will also (5) _____

_____.

My greatest hope for you is that (6)

_____

_____.

Love, _____

Modified by JT Fest for Youth Development: A Winning Hand
From original source: Fund for the City of New York, Youth Development Institute

If you have completed your letter, continue with Lesson 2.

Ignore your letter for now. You will be using it later in this lesson. But first, let's take a look at the categories of Youth Outcomes.

Achievement and Prevention Outcomes

Regardless of the specific manner in which you are working with young people, the outcomes to which you are most likely being held accountable will fall into one (or both) of two major categories. They will either be categorized as _Achievement_ Outcomes, or _Prevention_ Outcomes.

Achievement outcomes consist of things that result in tangible accomplishments. These are outcomes that you can _see_ and _count_, making measurement quite easy. If you have a school completion program, and 8 out of 10 participants complete school, your program is 80% successful. Put simply, achievement outcomes are an increase in desired accomplishments that can be seen and counted (e.g.; graduations, job attainment, securing stable housing).

If you are an employee of an agency or program, take a moment to list the specific achievement outcomes to which your position is held accountable. You may list as many as you wish, but list at least 3. If you are not an employee being held to specific outcomes, list at least 3 achievement outcomes that you wish to see for the young people with whom you interact. Do not read any further until you have completed this assignment.

If you have listed 3 or more achievement outcomes, continue with Lesson 2.

Prevention outcomes consist of changes in future behaviors, decisions, choices, or activities. They represent reductions in undesired things that _may_ occur. Prevention outcomes are less tangible than achievement outcomes, and are usually measured by comparison. For example, in 2012 the teen pregnancy rate in the United States was approximately 30% per 1,000 youth age 15-19 (according to the Centers for Disease Control and Prevention). But let's say that the teens in your pregnancy prevention program demonstrate a 15% rate. You can claim that your program is cutting teen pregnancy in half. Put simply, prevention outcomes are a decrease in undesired potential occurrences (e.g.; drug use/abuse, violence, dropping out of school).

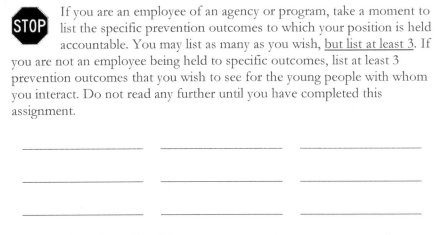

If you are an employee of an agency or program, take a moment to list the specific prevention outcomes to which your position is held accountable. You may list as many as you wish, but list at least 3. If you are not an employee being held to specific outcomes, list at least 3 prevention outcomes that you wish to see for the young people with whom you interact. Do not read any further until you have completed this assignment.

_____   _____   _____

_____   _____   _____

_____   _____   _____

If you have listed 3 or more prevention outcomes, continue with Lesson 2.

When discussing youth outcomes in terms of *achievement* or *prevention*, we are thinking in terms of the things that we *want* young people to do, or of the things that we *don't want* them to do, or both. This is the first and most significant way that the Youth Development approach differs from other youth work approaches. In the area of outcomes, Youth Development focuses on neither *achievement* nor *prevention*. Instead, it focuses on *development*.

IMPORTANT NOTE: Nothing in this lesson or elsewhere in this workbook is intended to replace, undermine, or challenge outcome goals of an agency, program, or school for which you may work. Rather, it is intended to enhance, support, and provide additional perspectives on those outcome goals. Always check with your supervisor regarding any conflicts you may perceive. Remember, Positive Youth Development is about modifying *how* you do things ... it is not about changing *what* you do.

Developmental Outcomes

<u>Developmental</u> outcomes refer to beliefs, behaviors, knowledge, and skills. Unlike achievement outcomes, which focus on accomplishment, or prevention outcomes, which focus on avoidance, developmental outcomes focus on how young people identify themselves through their belief systems and actions, as well as the personal resources a young person demonstrates in terms of knowledge and skills. Put simply, developmental outcomes are the positive development of beliefs, behaviors, knowledge and skills that prepare a young person for health and success in adolescence and adulthood.

As defined in Lesson 1, Youth Development is an approach to working with young people that fosters their innate capacity for resiliency and supports their developmental process, so the outcomes that PYD seeks are all related to a young person's healthy development. We are not focusing on what they do or don't do (or should or shouldn't do). Instead, we are focusing on *who and what they are becoming.*

The "Winning Hand" presentation refers to developmental outcomes as "DO's" as it reminds us that this is what we want to be "do"-ing. But the obvious question is, *do what?* With achievement and prevention outcomes, the answer is clear. Get a job, complete school, stay off drugs, don't be violent, etc. (you may refer back to the lists you previously created for addition outcomes). Outcomes related to achievement and prevention are for the most part clear and measurable -- but how do you measure success if you are targeting a young person's development? What are you trying to do, and how do you know that you're doing it?

There have been many attempts to answer this question. One of the earliest is the Montessori approach defining four "dimensions" of personality (emotional, moral, cognitive, and social) across four "planes" of development based on age (birth-6, 6-puberty, puberty-18, 18-24). A more well-known attempt within the field of Youth Development are the 40 Developmental Assets created by the Search Institute (search-institute.org). Another popular approach is the 5, 6, or sometimes 7 "C's." These "C's" represent *Competence* (academic, social, and vocational); *Confidence* (positive self-concept); *Connections* (to community, family, and peers); *Character* (positive values, integrity and moral values); and *Contributions* (active, meaningful roles in decision-making and facilitating change). Some researchers substitute *Caring* (positive regard for others) for *Contributions*, while others add it to the list as a 6th "C". The American Academy of Pediatrics adds *Coping* (positive coping strategies) and *Control* (internal) to the "basic 5" for a total of 7 "C's."

In fact, the need to establish some agreed upon outcomes and measures may be the greatest challenge facing the field of Positive Youth Development, but there is one saving grace. When you compare all of the various attempts to define developmental outcomes, it becomes quickly apparent that everyone is saying essentially the same thing. The package may be different depending on the author's own unique perspective, background, and approach, but as with the presentation of Protective Factors, the content always has more similarities than differences.

In terms of putting developmental outcomes into action, that is, turning the theory into practice with a concrete framework for outcomes that can be used to measure the success of your PYD efforts, I personally prefer the outcomes description originally developed for a youth worker training curriculum called Advancing Youth Development[5]. This curriculum defines 12 specific outcomes categorized under two major headings (see the Youth Outcomes Chart in Appendix B).

The first heading is **Aspects of Identity**, which lists outcomes that refer to *beliefs and behaviors* that create a sense of personal well-being, and a connection and commitment to others. These outcomes represent the "*who am I and where is my place in the world*" aspects of a young person's development.

The second heading is **Areas of Ability**, which lists outcomes that refer to specific *knowledge and skills* that give young people the ability and motivation for current and future success. These outcomes represent the "*what do I know, and what am I good at*" aspects of a young person's development. Together these lists provide a blueprint for outcome targets, but let's take a closer look at the 12 outcomes within these headings.

The Aspects of Identity heading refers to outcomes related to what a young person believes about themselves and their place in the world. It includes the six outcome targets of Self-worth, Safety and Structure, Belonging and Membership, Responsibility and Autonomy, Mastery and Future, and Self-awareness and Spirituality. These targets all reflect an ideal self-image.

For example, when the outcome of Self-worth is realized, you have a young person who thinks of themselves as a contributing, good person. With Mastery and Future, they believe themselves to be capable of success (however they may define success) with similar definitions for the remaining four outcomes. The idea here is that we are focusing on *belief systems* and *behaviors*, rather than what a young person is doing or not doing. But this is only part of the developmental picture.

We also need to look at their personal resources. The Areas of Ability heading refers to outcomes related to an individual's knowledge and skills, and includes the six outcome targets of Mental Health, Physical Health, Intellectual Ability, Employability, Civic and Social Ability and Cultural Ability. These targets all reflect an ideal level of competence.

It is important to understand that when we speak of knowledge and skills as a developmental outcome, we are referring to an individual's *ability and motivation*. This is a critical distinction that separates *developmental* outcomes from *achievement* outcomes. For example, when we look at the developmental outcome of employability, it is easy to confuse that outcome with getting a job. However, getting a job is an *achievement* outcome. The *developmental* outcome of employability refers to possessing the *ability* and the *motivation* to get a job. Granted, if a young person has the ability and motivation to get a job, the likely result is that they will become employed. But when focusing on developmental outcomes, getting a job is a happy *consequence* of success rather than its *measurement*.

By focusing on ability and motivation, Areas of Ability prepares young people for long-term success, as opposed to short-term achievements. This specific focus defines all of the outcomes under this heading and is the key to understanding the difference between a developmental focus on knowledge and skills, and the achievement/prevention focus that may appear to be virtually the same thing. The idea here is that we are focusing on possessing ability and motivation as opposed to accomplishing any specific goal or the actual application of ability.

The danger of discussing these headings as separate lists is that we can easily fall into one of the major "don'ts" of DO's, and that is, don't think of them as autonomous goals. We separate them into Aspects of Identity and Areas of Ability for clarity, but not for practice. The 12 outcomes are not a list of options to pick and choose among, but rather are a holistic target for an individual's healthy development. Specific programs may focus on one outcome as a priority (for example, a school completion program may prioritize Intellectual Ability), but all 12 should receive some level of attention if we hope to ensure current and future success.

Take Aspects of Identity for example. These outcomes are similar to the outcome goals of many self-esteem programs, but the question is, how long will these beliefs last if you don't know how to function in the world?

Likewise, Areas of Ability may be similar to many outcome goals of skill-based programs, but here the question is, what good are these skills if you feel that you are worthless and undeserving? Focusing on developmental outcomes is a commitment to seeing the complete young person, rather than just a specific problem or deficit.

As already mentioned, the Advancing Youth Development curriculum provides only one of many approaches to defining developmental outcomes. Regardless of the definition that works for you, the concept remains that you are focusing *more* on who and what a young person is becoming, and *less* on what they are doing or not doing.

Challenges to Developmental Outcomes

It should be noted that a focus on developmental outcomes is not without its critics. There are those who strongly believe that psycho-emotional and/or behavioral problems require an achievement or prevention approach. But the theory of Positive Youth Development is that a young person's apparent problems or deficits are simply *symptoms* of unmet developmental needs, and that a focus on developmental outcomes is actually more effective since it addresses root *causes* rather than surface *issues*. This may be why there is evidence of improved outcomes through Positive Youth Development[6], because the approach focuses on causes, not symptoms.

A second criticism is that achievement and prevention outcomes are *important*. It's important that young people succeed in school, get jobs, stay off of drugs, and refrain from violence. In fact, if you are an employee of an agency, program, or school it is possible that your performance is being evaluated based on your ability to move young people toward specific achievement and/or prevention outcomes. Here, Positive Youth Development agrees with its critics, but PYD takes it a step further and believes that these things are *too* important to make them our focus, as we will simply be realizing short-term results. By assisting young people in their developmental process, we obtain a lifetime of self-motivated achievement and prevention. Developmental outcomes *result* in achievement and prevention outcomes, but as a *consequence* instead of as a *goal*. A young person with the beliefs, behaviors, knowledge, and skills resulting from developmental outcomes is unlikely to be under-achieving or engaging in risk behaviors. This is why you can use a PYD approach focusing on developmental outcomes even if your performance is evaluated on achievement and prevention outcomes, because your success with DO's *results* in achievement and prevention.

There's an analogy that I find helpful. Let's compare outcomes to wanting to fill your house with flowers. There are two ways you can go. You can bring in cut flowers, which have the advantage of being attractive and very easy to get. The problem is that they are generally expensive and don't last very long. After a few days they fade away and, in order to keep flowers in your house, you have to go out, invest more money, and bring in more cut flowers. Your other option would be potted plants. It's true that they sometimes require a greater investment in time and energy. They need to be nurtured and watered, and sometimes transplanted. But they are generally cheaper in the long run and, once they begin to bloom, you have flowers for years to come (perennially speaking).

Achievement and prevention outcomes are the cut flowers of the outcome world. They look good, and they are relatively easy to get. All you have to do is control the young person's choices and actions, and you get the outcomes you are seeking. But what happens in the future, when the young person is responsible for controlling their *own* choices and actions? We might hope that they have learned from their experience, but we often see that they have only learned to do what they're told. This is why we see young people do well in programs, and revert back to pre-program problems and behaviors when they leave (known in the field as *recidivism*).

Developmental outcomes are the potted plants of the outcome world. It can be more challenging to focus on a young person's developmental needs instead of their problems, but it is also more rewarding. Young people learn to govern their own choices and actions in healthy and responsible ways, resulting in change that is permanent and setting the stage for a lifetime of success. For additional perspective on this, see "An Outlook on Outcomes," part of the Bonus Lesson: Measuring Developmental Outcomes, in Appendix A.

A third criticism is that developmental outcomes are not practical for programs and agencies to implement because staff has difficulty understanding what they are. Staff can understand getting off drugs, or getting a job, or not getting pregnant … but how do we expect people to "get" developmental outcomes? I challenge this criticism as being unfounded, and I'm going to ask you to help me prove my point.

 Before you proceed: Review the letter you wrote in the previous assignment. Follow the instructions on the next page and complete this assignment before continuing with Lesson 2.

Instructions: Review the letter you wrote. You will notice that the lines of your letter are numbered 1 through 6. Consider each of your responses individually, beginning with line #1.

Consider what you wrote on line #1. What are you talking about? Maybe you're referring to strength, or community, or occupation. It doesn't matter what it is, but it is important that you identify the *concept* in a single word or short phrase. Once you have determined and are able to express the concept of what you were talking about on line #1, turn to Appendix B and look at the Youth Outcomes Chart.

This chart describes developmental outcomes (as modified from the Advancing Youth Development curriculum), as well as achievement and prevention outcomes. Read them and determine which one of the 14 outcomes listed is the closest match to what you were talking about on line #1. It doesn't have to be an exact match, just the closest fit. Were you talking about an achievement outcome? *Put a "1" in the achievement outcome box.* Were you talking about Mastery and Future? *Put a "1" in the Mastery and Future box.* When you have put "1" on the chart, repeat this procedure for each of the remaining 5 lines in your letter, until 1-6 is on the chart.

GO Upon completion of this assignment, review your results. It is highly likely that the majority of your numbers were placed on a developmental outcome, as opposed to an achievement or prevention outcome. The question is; *how is this possible?*

When you wrote your letter, we had not yet discussed outcomes *at all*. You were simply asked to describe what your hopes were for a young person that you personally cared about. Despite the fact that we had not yet discussed developmental outcomes, you already had an idea about what they were and held them in higher regard than achievement or prevention outcomes. Below is the letter that you probably did *not* write.

Dear Little *problem child*

Welcome to the world! I hope that you grow up to be *a law-abiding citizen.* I want you to experience *individual and group counseling* and to always *modify your behavior to community standards.* I know that you will learn to *restrain yourself from violent outbursts* and will also *use appropriate language and avoid sexual activity.* My greatest hope for you is that *you stay off of drugs, get a high school diploma or GED, and receive vocational training.*

Why was your letter so different? This letter certainly reflects the focus of most youth programs, yet it doesn't reflect *your* focus when you thought about an individual young person you cared about. The fact that it doesn't destroys the myth that developmental outcomes are difficult for people to learn. They're not difficult, because most people *already* know them. It is simply a matter of putting your intuitive knowledge into words, and modifying your approach to the youth *in your care* to be similar to the approach that you have to the youth that *you care about*. This, incidentally, ties into the "caring" qualifier of the Caring and Supportive Relationships Protective Factor (Lesson 6).

There is one final criticism that is often cited; that developmental outcomes are difficult to *measure*. This criticism is addressed in Appendix A: Bonus Lesson: Measuring Developmental Outcomes.

Summation

- Outcomes are the "bottom line" of youth work. Regardless of the *model* of youth work in which you are engaged, the outcomes that result from your work are the most important part of your practice.
- Outcomes fall into three major categories: achievement, prevention, and developmental.
- Achievement outcomes are an increase in desired accomplishments that can be seen and counted.
- Prevention outcomes are a decrease in undesired potential occurrences.
- Developmental outcomes are beliefs, behaviors, knowledge and skills that prepare a young person for a successful adolescence and adulthood.
- Most youth work approaches focus on achievement or prevention outcomes; that is, they are concerned with what a young person should or shouldn't be doing.
- Youth Development focuses on developmental outcomes; that is, it is concerned with who and what a young person is becoming.
- Within the Youth Development field there is not yet agreement on a specific way to define developmental outcomes. The four primary efforts in this regard are the Montessori approach, the Search Institute's 40 Developmental Assets, the 5 (or 6 or 7) C's, and the Advancing Youth Development curriculum.
- These multiple efforts tend to have more similarities than differences. The *concept* is to focus *more* on who and what a young person is becoming, and *less* on what they are doing or not doing.
- Youth Development values achievement and prevention, but sees these outcomes as a consequence, rather than a goal.

Learning Assignment 2
Complete **BEFORE** proceeding

Part 1: Interview your youth learning partner(s) and ask:

1. What attracts you to programs or activities and keeps you engaged?

---

2. What can adults do to help you "make it," specifically, what are five (5) things that adults can do to help you succeed? **NOTE:** Allow the young person(s) to use their own definition of "success." Be prepared to explain your terminology if needed.

Part 2: <u>After</u> completing Part 1, meet with your supervisor (or adult learning partner) and discuss the following questions. Write the key points of your discussion below:

1. What did you learn from Lesson 2 and/or your interview(s) that was new for you?

---

2. What did you re-learn or remember as a result of Lesson 2 and/or your interview(s)?

_____

_____

_____

3. List the key thoughts, points, or ideas that you want to remember from Lesson 2 and/or your interview(s). You may list as many items as you wish, but list at least 3.

_____

_____

_____

GO If you have completed Parts 1, and 2 of Learning Assignment 2, you may now move on to Lesson 3.

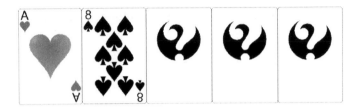

Lesson 3
(s)OS: A Framework for Youth Development

*Too often we give our children answers to remember
rather than problems to solve.*

~ *Roger Lewin* ~

In this lesson you will learn:

- Lesson Anchor: The Eight of Spades
- (s)OS: (services), Opportunities and Supports

Lesson Anchor: The Eight of Spades

The second card in your Winning Hand is the **Eight of Spades**. Please draw it now and place it with your Ace of Hearts from Lesson 2, which should be a location where you see it often. This is the anchor card for **Lesson 3 -- (s)OS: A framework for Youth Development**.

The "8" was selected because, when viewed horizontally, it resembles the recognized symbol of *infinity*, a concept that means *without end*. The suit of spades was selected for an idiomatic usage of the term. You've heard of doing something *in spades*. When used idiomatically like this, *in spades* means *to a considerable degree*. If you are doing something *in spades*, you are doing it *a lot*.

As you begin this lesson, remember that the **Ace of Hearts** reminds you that outcomes are the "Bottom Line" of youth work, and that you know in your heart what young people need to develop into healthy and successful adolescents and adults (DO's, or Developmental Outcomes.). Now, to successfully implement the Youth Development approach, the **Eight of**

26

Spades reminds you to take the framework presented in this lesson and use it *to a considerable degree, without end* (do it *in spades* for *infinity*).

(s)OS: (services), Opportunities and Supports

This lesson provides the framework for implementing a Youth Development approach. This is a framework to be utilized in your daily practice as you focus on developmental outcomes (DO's), and it is within this framework that you will create the Protective Factor environments that will foster a young person's innate capacity for resiliency (these Protective Factors are further explored in Lesson's 4, 5, and 6). The framework is called **(services), Opportunities and Supports,** or **(s)OS** and there are two immediate points that need to be clarified.

The first is that the (s), or (services), is not capitalized and presented in parenthesis *intentionally*. The intention is to emphasize a specific point concerning services which will be explained in the next section. The second is that (s)OS represents *two*, not *three*, concepts. The OS, which stands for Opportunities and Supports, is presented here as *joined together*, again, with *intention*. The importance of these two points will be expanded upon as (s)OS is further defined.

All of the concepts within the (s)OS framework refer to a specific form of practice within the Youth Development approach. The point has been made throughout this workbook that PYD is an *approach*, not a *model*. PYD is not *what* you do (that is defined by your relationship, job, and/or program model); it is *how* you do it. (s)OS gives you a framework for *how* you do *what* you do. Understanding this concept is central to understanding the *practice* of Positive Youth Development.

(s), or (services)

There is a simple way to identify if a specific activity is a (service). Look at the activity through a word filter consisting of *to* or *for*. In other words, if you are doing something *to* or *for* a young person, you are providing a (service). You apply assessment criterion *to* a young person; you make a phone call *for* a young person; you assign an area of study *to* a young person; you grade papers *for* a young person -- all of these activities are able to be expressed as being done *to* or *for* a young person, and therefore they all are considered to be a (service).

They also represent the bulk of what takes place within the youth service field. The field itself, in fact, is called youth *services*. There is nothing wrong with providing (services) per se, ~~but we should always be aware that when we are providing (services), that is, when we are doing *to* or *for*, we are not promoting development~~. We may be promoting many positive things (safety, support), but *development* is not one of them.

This is why (services) is represented without capitals and within parenthesis -- to reinforce the concept that (services) are not Youth Development. The question then becomes, why include (services) in our framework at all? The answer is that while (services) are not Youth Development, they are often an important foundation in *support* of Youth Development. A small digression is required to make this point.

Consider the theory of personality defined by humanistic psychologist Abraham Maslow, commonly referred to as Maslow's "Hierarchy of Needs[7]." Maslow theorized that human beings have instinctual basic needs that must be actualized *in sequence* as a person grows and develops. In other words, a person will not seek to satisfy the second need until the first need has been satisfied, and so on. While this is probably a review for most of you, we often need reminding as much as we need educating.

Maslow's Hierarchy consists of five basic needs, generally shown as a pyramid, with the base of the pyramid being the first need that must be satisfied before the next "level" of needs is pursued. While "higher" levels of needs, such as spiritual needs, exist beyond the pyramid, the majority of our choices and decisions are motivated by a desire to satisfy these five needs in order. Beginning with the base, these needs are:

1. Physiological Needs
   We can also think of these as biological needs, such as the need for oxygen, food and water.

2. Safety Needs
   This is our need to feel safe in the world, and believe that our environment is stable and secure.

3. Love and Belonging Needs
   Human beings are social creatures, and we seek to overcome feelings of loneliness and alienation. We look for ways to give and receive love and affection and to form bonds and attachments that give us a sense of belonging.

4. Esteem Needs
   Human beings need to feel self-confident, valuable, and valued. Esteem needs refers to both self-esteem as well as the esteem we receive from others.

5. Self-Actualization Needs
   This level of needs was described by Maslow as our need to be and do that which we were "born to do." It is our inner motivation to discover and become who we are "meant to be" in this life.

Refer back to Lesson 1 where we discussed the concept and practice definitions of Youth Development, and you will see that Youth Development is fully compatible with Maslow's theory. Youth Development describes our desire to satisfy Maslow's "needs" as an on-going *process* of seeking ways to meet our basic physical (physiological) and social (safety, love and belonging) needs while building competencies (esteem and self-actualization). It is relatively easy to relate the higher levels of Maslow's pyramid to the developmental outcomes (DO's) on which we focus when implementing a Youth Development approach. But Youth Development has difficulty with the first level of the pyramid. Certain populations of young people (street-dependent youth, for example) may have significant aspects of their lives still stuck at a basic physiological level, and it is very difficult to focus on developmental outcomes with a young person whose basic physiological needs are inadequately met.

This defines the need for (services) as a foundation for a Youth Development approach. Where basic needs are inadequately met or young people do not have the required level of skills or resources to meet their own needs, (services) may be required as a base upon which to build. But since (services) are not Youth Development, they should be seen as *minimal necessary interventions*. The major focus of your approach should be on creating opportunities and providing supports. That said, the reality is that most youth services, from street outreach to a traditional classroom, have too much to accomplish and not enough resources. There will be many aspects of the "what you do" that, for various reasons, it may not be practical to not provide as a (service). It's not that doing *to* or *for* is a bad thing to be avoided … it's that it doesn't contribute to a youth's *development*, and activities that do (Opportunities and Supports) should be *maximized*.

OS, or Opportunities and Supports

Remember that we are discussing joined concepts here. While I will define Opportunities and Supports separately, you should see it as similar to describing two sides of a coin. The descriptions may vary somewhat, but you're talking about the same, single coin, and you can't have one side without the other. One of the factors that often interferes with a successful implementation of PYD is that, unlike a coin, you *can* separate Opportunities and Supports, providing one without providing the other. However, no matter how well you do with each individually it is only when they are joined together that they are effective from a Youth Development perspective.

Opportunities

 Follow the instructions below and complete the exercise. Do **NOT** read any further until after you have completed the exercise.

Instructions: Imagine that you work for Area 51 and have the task of teaching human concepts to a visitor from another planet. While making small talk on a hot day you casually mention that it would be a good day for ice cream. The alien tilts its head and curiously asks; what is "ice cream?" Realizing that the alien has never heard of, seen, or had any previous knowledge of ice cream, it is your challenge to explain exactly what the human concept of ice cream entails. Develop your explanation by filling out the following form. **Note**: This is not a test. You do not have to research ice cream and answer every question correctly. From your knowledge and in your own words, simply answer as best as you are able.

What is ice cream made of (ingredients)?

_____

_____

_____

What flavors does ice cream come in?

_____

_____

_____

Why do people eat ice cream?

_____

_____

_____

Are there any "down sides" to eating ice cream?

_____

_____

_____

GO The answers you wrote in your ice cream description may not be an exact match for the answers that follow, but it is likely that they are very similar. You probably listed such things as cream, sugar, eggs, ice, milk, or just some general references to dairy and cold as you described the ingredients. For flavors, you may have hit the Big Three (chocolate, vanilla, and strawberry), but you may have simply stated that there is an unlimited number of flavors that can go into ice cream (fans of the Food Network's Iron Chef probably remember Chef Sakai's infamous *trout* ice cream). As for why we eat ice cream, you probably didn't list "nutritional value" as one of your reasons. More likely you talked about it being a treat, a comfort food, or a way to keep cool on a hot day. In the "down side" area, you may have talked about weight gain, or perhaps the strange phenomenon of "brain freeze."

No matter how you answered the questions, you undoubtedly ended up with a detailed, complete, and accurate description of ice cream. Now I have another question for you. After giving your description to the alien, does the creature have any *real* concept of what ice cream is? My guess is that you just answered "no." Given that, I have one last question for you. What would the creature have to do in order to *truly* understand ice cream?

That's right. The alien would have to *try* some.

If you understand this, then you understand the theory behind Opportunities. You can talk to young people about responsibility until you are blue in the face. They won't understand what you are talking about until they experience *being* responsible. You can discuss leadership with young people until the cows come home. They won't understand what you're talking about until they are in a position to *be* a leader. Opportunities are circumstances that give young people *direct* experience.

There is also a word filter that will identify if a specific activity is an Opportunity. In this case, the word filter is *by*. Things that are done *by* young people are Opportunities, but there is a certain level of honesty that needs to be part of this word filter. It is easy to put 30 youth in a classroom, tell them to open their books to chapter three and read, and identify that the activity is being done *by* young people. This is not an Opportunity, however, because while they may be taking the action, they are really only doing what they have been told to do. For an activity to be an Opportunity there must be a direct link to the *choice* and *responsibility* for the action. It must be an act of *volition*.

Opportunities are chances for young people to act in or on the world around them; to explore, express, experience, experiment, and influence. But there is a critical piece of understanding that goes with creating Opportunities for young people, and this understanding is one of the keys to successful Youth Development implementation.

Consider for a moment the following scenario. A young person who has never in their life had the opportunity to be involved in a specific task or function is given such an opportunity. What might be a potential outcome of this scenario? You have to admit that a potential, perhaps even a probable outcome is that the young person will *fail* in that task or function. You almost never do something *new* correctly the *first time* you try. This is where we see many attempts at PYD fall apart; when trying to include young people as participants, the young people *fail to demonstrate success*, and we conclude that *PYD* has failed and go back to a more directive, authoritarian approach.

But the fact is that in this scenario, failure is not a problem, it is *success*. This is how people grow and learn; by trying something, failing, learning from the failure, and trying again. If we protect young people from this process, *we delay their development*, and sooner or later they will have to go through the experience of failure, learning, and growth. Youth Development is an approach that goes through that process *with* them, rather than *delay* that process for them. In fact, an argument can be made that an issue with many youth services today is an institutional *bias toward success*. By protecting young people from failure we help them succeed with short-term program goals, but delay the growth that comes from failing until after they leave the program. By viewing success as a long-term goal that is achieved through trial and error, programs can help young people through the difficult developmental stages that are the *prerequisite* for a healthy and accomplished life. We accomplish that by looking at the other side of the coin: Supports.

Supports

The word filter that identifies a Support is *with*. We work *with* young people in relationship to a specific Opportunity to provide the support needed for a successful outcome. A "successful outcome" does not mean that the *young person* was successful, though it certainly doesn't preclude that possibility. However, when we speak of success in this context, we are focused on the young person's *development*. If they have grown and learned from the Opportunity, we have a successful outcome -- even if the Opportunity itself might be seen as a "failure."

Supports are interpersonal relationships and resources. They are people, information, and material needs that ensure that a young person grows and learns from Opportunities.

Pulling Them Apart

Remember that Opportunities and Supports are a joined concept. Separating them from each other eliminates their function as a framework for Youth Development. If you provide an Opportunity without a corresponding Support, you have simply set the young person up for failure without growth. An example would be putting a young person on an agency Board of Directors by simply pulling another chair up to the table. While it is a great opportunity for the young person, how many young people have ever met under Robert's Rules of Order, or read an agency budget report? Without the corresponding support of having people and information available for them to understand how the Board functions, it is likely to be an unpleasant experience for all involved.

By the same token, if you provide a Support without a corresponding Opportunity, all you really have is adult directed activity. It is nearly impossible to act *with* young people if there is nothing being done *by* young people.

Putting Them Together

One of the best ways to visualize Opportunities and Supports is to think of how you teach someone to drive. Do you get behind the wheel and drive them around? Not if you want them to *learn*. If learning is your goal, *they* get behind the wheel and you sit in the passenger's seat, offering guidance, information, and feedback. Now, why do you teach someone to drive using someone else's car and practicing in a big, empty Wal-Mart parking lot? It's because when they are first learning, you _know_ that they are going to make mistakes. They will accelerate too fast, brake too hard, turn too wide, and pop the clutch. When this happens, do you conclude that they are incapable of driving and take over the driving for them? No. You provide guidance, information, and feedback as they grow, learn, and eventually become a competent driver.

The Framework

This is how you implement a Youth Development approach. You *minimize* services and *maximize* Opportunities and Supports. More to the point, you identify what you are doing *to* and *for* young people and, wherever possible, change that activity into something being done *by* young people *with* your support.

The traditional framework for youth work is to provide success-biased services that result in achievement and prevention outcomes. The Youth Development framework is to create Opportunities and provide Supports, allowing for both success and failure to contribute to a young person's growth and development.

In Lesson 2 we learned that, according to Youth Development theory, problems and challenges experienced by young people are theorized to be *effects* or *symptoms* of unmet developmental needs. The approach changes the focus of intervention away from the *symptom* (problems) and toward the *root cause* (developmental needs). While the concept of Youth Development is compatible with Maslow's theories, the practice of Youth Development requires that we shift our *thoughts* and *actions* away from the problem-oriented focus of traditional approaches to youth services. No longer is our measurement of success how well we "fix" or "correct" a young person's behaviors. Instead, our focus is solely on assisting young people in their development. This change in focus is based upon two significant assertions (beliefs). First, that an absence of problems in a young person's life does not indicate a child or adolescent prepared for or on the path to success in adulthood, nor does the presence of problems indicate a young person who is incompetent, incapable, or innately "bad." Second, that addressing identified problems by preventing or correcting them does not in and of itself promote healthy development.

A major advantage of this change in focus is that it allows us to move from the controlling and punitive models of care that working from a deficit or problem prevention perspective often requires, where we must constantly send messages about what a young person should or should not do, believe, or be. Instead, Youth Development allows us to focus on a young person's *potential*, helping them to realize what they *can* do, what the possibilities are, and who they can become.

Summation

- Implementing a Youth Development approach requires a consistent application of the (s)OS framework.
- (s)OS stands for (services) and *Opportunities and Supports*.
- A (service) is something you do *to* or *for* a young person, and (services) do not promote development, but may be a necessary foundation for activities that do promote development.
- *Opportunities and Supports* are actions *by* young people *with* adult support.
- A Youth Development approach is to reduce (services) to minimum required interventions and replace them with *Opportunities and Supports*. The goal is not success or failure, but growth and development.
- Traditional youth work provides success-biased services that result in achievement and prevention outcomes. Positive Youth Development creates Opportunities and provides Supports, allowing for both success and failure to contribute to a young person's growth and development.

STOP **Learning Assignment 3**
Complete **BEFORE** proceeding

Part 1: The Positive Youth Development approach utilizes the framework of (services), Opportunities and Supports to create Protective Factor environments that foster a young person's innate resiliency and promote their development. The final 3 lessons in this workbook take a deeper look at those Protective Factors. In preparation for these lessons, interview your youth learning partner(s), allowing them to use their own definition for words like "respect" and "care" (be prepared to explain your terminology if needed), and ask:

1. What do adults do that feels disrespectful to you?

_____

_____

_____

2. How do you feel and act when you perceive that adults are not respecting you?

_____

_____

_____

3. What are the specific personal attributes and behaviors that demonstrate "respect" and "caring?"

_____

_____

_____

4. How do you feel and act when you perceive that adults care about you and are treating you with respect?

_____

_____

_____

Part 2: <u>After</u> completing Part 1, meet with your supervisor (or adult learning partner) and discuss the following questions. Write the key points of your discussion below:

1. What did you learn from Lesson 3 and/or your interview(s) that was new for you?

_____

_____

_____

2. What did you re-learn or remember as a result of Lesson 3 and/or your interview(s)?

_____

_____

_____

3. List the key thoughts, points, or ideas that you want to remember from Lesson 3 and/or your interview(s). You may list as many items as you wish, but list at least <u>3</u>.

_____

_____

_____

GO <u>If you have completed Parts 1, and 2 of Learning Assignment 3,</u> you may now move on to Lesson 4.

Lesson 4
High Expectations

If we treat people as we find them, we may make them worse.
If we treat people as they ought to be, we help them become
what they are capable of becoming.

~ *Johann Wolfgang von Goethe* ~
(also attributed to Dr. Haim Ginott)

In this lesson you will learn:

- Lesson Anchor: Joker
- The challenge of High Expectations

Lesson Anchor: Joker

The third card in your Winning Hand is the **Joker**[8]. Please draw it now and place it with your Ace of Hearts from Lesson 2 and your Eight of Spades from Lesson 3, which should be a location where you see it often. This is the anchor card for **Lesson 4 -- High Expectations**.

The Joker is a unique card in all decks that most of us simply discard or set aside. You may wonder why decks of cards have Jokers at all, and prior to the mid-1800's, they didn't. Jokers were inserted into decks specifically to be used in the game of Euchre, a game with its roots in Germany where it was spelled Jucker (which is thought to have evolved in the United States to "Joker," hence the name of the card). It was intended to be the highest trump card in that game ... nothing beats the Joker.

The Joker is the perfect representation for this lesson. A card that is often unused and overlooked, yet it's there because of a game where it's the most powerful card in the deck. High Expectations have a similar identity in that we don't often focus on what our beliefs and expectations really are, or how they are communicated in our practice, but they are the "highest trump" in the "game" of Positive Youth Development.

As you begin this lesson, remember that the **Ace of Hearts** reminds you that outcomes are the "Bottom Line" of youth work, and that you know in your heart what young people need to develop into healthy and successful adolescents and adults (DO's, or Developmental Outcomes.). The **Eight of Spades** reminds you that the framework for the Youth Development approach, is to *minimize* services (*to* or *for*) and to *maximize* Opportunities and Supports (*by* and *with*) which should be applied *to a considerable degree, without end* (*in spades* for *infinity*). Now, to begin to build Protective Factors that will foster resiliency into that framework, the **Joker** reminds you to take the information presented in this lesson and use it as your "trump card." *Nothing* beats High Expectations.

We Begin with a Story

DHMO is colorless, odorless, tasteless, and kills thousands of people every year. Most of these deaths are caused by accidental inhalation, but inhalation of DHMO is not the only danger it poses. Prolonged exposure to its solid form causes severe tissue damage. Symptoms of DHMO ingestion can include excessive sweating and urination, nausea, vomiting, electrolyte imbalance, and even death.

DHMO, or Dihydrogen Monoxide, is the major component of acid rain. It contributes to the "greenhouse" effect, causes severe burns in its gaseous state, accelerates corrosion and rusting of many metals, and has been found in the excised tumors of terminal cancer patients. If you're not concerned yet, consider this; DHMO is found in every stream, lake, and reservoir in the world today. That's right, the pollution is global, and DHMO is even found in Antarctic ice.

Despite these dangers, DHMO is in use today as an industrial solvent and coolant, in nuclear power plants, in the production of Styrofoam, as a fire retardant, and in the distribution of pesticides. Even after washing, contaminated produce will retain trace levels of DHMO.

When presented with these facts the public is consistent in their response. Dozens of petitions have been circulated calling for a complete and total ban on DHMO, and these petitions routinely demonstrate public support in the 80% range or higher. There was even a vote scheduled in the California municipality of Aliso Viejo (an Orange County suburb) for a proposed law to ban the use of foam containers at city-sponsored events due to the fact that DHMO is used in the production of these containers, citing a "threat to human health and safety[9]."

The vote was cancelled once it was revealed to the city council the true nature of DHMO. As it turns out, dihydrogen (or, two hydrogen atoms ... H_2) monoxide (or, one oxygen atom ... O), is *water* (H_2O).

It needs to be pointed out that all of the information I provided above is absolutely factual. Water does kill thousands of people every year through accidental inhalation (it's called "drowning). Prolonged exposure to its solid form (ice) will cause severe tissue damage. Water is the major component of acid rain and does contribute to the "greenhouse" effect. In its gaseous state (steam) it will cause severe burns. Additionally, water does accelerate corrosion and rusting of metals, and it has been found in the excised tumors of terminal cancer patients (water is in every cell in the body, healthy or not).

What's the point? The point is that we are human beings, and as human beings we are "hard wired" to react in certain ways. Lesson 1 discussed the research conclusion that we are "hard wired" to be innately capable of resilient behavior. We are also "hard wired" with a will to survive (if you doubt this, remember the story of hiker Aron Ralston who was trapped in the wilderness when his arm got stuck under a boulder. With no hope of rescue, *he amputated his own arm with a pocketknife* in order to survive). When faced with danger, we are "hard wired" to go into a *fight or flight*[10] response. In a similar manner, we are somewhat "hard wired" in the way that we deal with information.

There is so much information for us to process these days that we are literally incapable of critically thinking about each and every piece of information that comes our way. The result is that we develop "tapes" that we play and, when information fits, we tend to stop thinking and simply "play the tape." This is what happens when people are asked to sign a petition banning DHMO. We are provided with just enough information to trigger our "chemicals in the environment are bad" tape and we start thinking about pollution and oil spills and toxic dumps and we sign our name. But the truth is that chemicals *are* the environment and, if you were to react from an informed position, you would need a lot more information about DHMO than the petitions provide (like, the fact that it is water and that we would all die without it, for example).

Another way in which we are "hard wired" is that, for whatever reason, we tend to accept the negative and question the positive. Try to give someone a compliment and see how hard it is for them to accept. Yet, let them hear you say something negative about them and I promise you that they'll take it to heart. One theory is that this is the result of human evolution. An early human out in the Serengeti hears a rustling in the weeds. The pessimistic negative thinker fears that it is a predator and changes their path. The optimistic positive thinker dismisses it as wind and walks into the weeds. There will be times, however, when it *was* a predator, not the wind. Over time, the pessimistic negative thinkers survive and reproduce, while the optimistic positive thinkers slowly die off as tasty treats for weed-hidden predators.

Regardless of how it came about, human beings tend to give greater credence to negative presentations. A petition asking you to legalize a chemical and touting its benefits will no doubt be met with skepticism, but a petition asking for a ban and touting danger is more often than not simply signed.

What does all of this have to do with High Expectations? Simply that the greatest challenge we face when implementing a Youth Development approach has nothing to do with young people. The challenge is *personal*, and has to do with our beliefs and expectations about young people, *which have a direct impact upon the young people with whom we interact.* High Expectations are a Protective Factor that fosters the innate capacity for resiliency. Low Expectations are a Risk Factor that inhibits the innate capacity for resiliency. Most of our "tapes" related to young people are negative, and communicate low rather than high expectations.

 Follow the instructions on the next page and complete the exercise. Do **NOT** read any further until after you have completed the exercise.

Instructions: Depending on your specific situation, this exercise may take you several hours or several days. Additionally, it requires you to enlist the aid of colleagues or friends. Below are several different labels. Select a label, print or type it on a post-it note and attach it to yourself where others can see it. For example, you may put it on your shirt, or even your forehead.

Then:

1. Tell the people around you that you are conducting an experiment and ask them to participate.

2. Select a period of time and inform them of the length. For example, it may be for the duration of a staff meeting, or maybe for the next half hour while having lunch. The setting, people, and duration are up to you, but make sure that you request and get cooperation.

3. Tell your participant(s) to read your label and, for the duration of the exercise, *treat you and speak to you as though this is what they truly believe about you*. The better that they do this, the more accurate will be the results. Give them permission to be as true to this belief about you as possible.

Labels:

I'm a little slow	I may get violent	Just ignore me	I need therapy

You may conduct this exercise as many times as you wish using the same or different labels. When you feel you have a familiarity with the experience, complete the questions on the next page.

Overall, what was this experience like for you?

_____

_____

_____

What did you feel *emotionally* when you were being treated as labeled?

_____

_____

_____

What were your *thoughts* as you were being treated as labeled?

_____

_____

_____

How did you *respond* or *act* while being treated as labeled?

_____

_____

GO If you are like most people, you probably didn't enjoy this exercise. No one likes to be treated according to a preconceived notion about who they are or what they are capable of doing. If your partners in this exercise played their roles well, you may have noticed something else disconcerting. You may have noticed that some of your feelings, thoughts, or reactions actually *conformed* to the belief system. You may have withdrawn when ignored, or started wondering what was wrong with you when you needed therapy, or started acting a little slow when people thought you were a little slow, or started getting agitated when people were treating you as though you might become violent.

What you experienced is a research-backed reaction known as the *Pygmalion Effect*. While there have been numerous experiments confirming this effect, the original was conducted by Robert Rosenthal and Lenore Jacobson[11]. In their experiment, they randomly selected a segment of students and told the teachers that based on tests they conducted these students were "intellectual bloomers" and could be expected to show remarkable gains during the year. The result of their experiment was that the randomly selected students showed non-random progress above and beyond their peers. This progress was not because the students were in any way different from their peers, but rather because their teachers *believed* that they were different.

Here's how the Pygmalion Effect works. We have certain beliefs or expectations about people. We communicate these beliefs and expectations with various cues, mostly without *intention* to do so. Our tone of voice, our body language, what we choose to say or not say, and what we choose to pay attention to or ignore all communicate our beliefs and expectations. People receiving these cues respond to them, and begin to adjust their behavior to match the cues that they are receiving. Their behavior then confirms and reinforces our pre-conceived beliefs, and the cycle strengthens and continues. The result is that our beliefs and expectations about people become "true" -- a kind of self-fulfilling prophesy.

This is why our beliefs and expectations need to be examined and communicated with *intention*. They will motivate how young people respond to us. If you believe that you are working with young people who are disruptive, resistant, and unwilling to participate, you will find yourself working with young people who are disruptive, resistant, and unwilling to participate. If you believe that you are working with young people who are competent, capable, and eager to contribute, you will find yourself working with young people who are competent, capable, and eager to contribute. The single most important factor in our impact on young people ... our "highest trump card" ... is the beliefs and expectations that the involved adults have about the youth with whom they are working.

I had a personal experience that underscores this point. I was consulting with a new group home program that was being developed for street-dependent youth. They had formed a Board, found a facility, and hired staff, and they were eager to begin taking in residents. What they had not done, in my opinion, was develop the program sufficiently, so I suggested that they do a "trial run." I asked if they would budget money for me to hire some youth consultants. The consultants would "move in" to the program as though they were the first residents, live there and experience the program from a young person's perspective for 3 days, and then report to the staff and Board on what they found helpful, and offer ideas for improvement.

The trial run was approved and the youth consultants were retained. Three days later, the feedback meeting was held and the youth consultants gave what everyone agreed were some extremely helpful and insightful suggestions. After the meeting ended, as we were all saying goodbye, one of the Board members made the following statement to me:

"I want to thank you and your youth consultants, but I'm not sure that this was a realistic test for our program."

When I asked why, she stated:

"Because your youth consultants are obviously exceptional young people, and I don't think that they're typical of the population we're going to see here."

So, let me tell you about my youth consultants.

They were 2 males and 2 females, all age 17. One of the females was an on and off resident of an emergency shelter I operated. In fact, I had done no less than 10 interventions concerning violence with her, as she had a reputation for being one of the most violent young women in that system. The other young woman had bombed out of every housing and shelter program in a tri-county area and wanted to be involved in this project as she had just again lost her place to live and needed a place to stay. The two young men I can't really tell you that much about, as I stopped at a drop-in center on the way out of town and pretty much picked these guys up off of the floor, filling them in about the project on the drive to the program.

My "youth consultants" were absolutely typical of the population. They were the difficult, drug-affected, "problem" youth in a different system. A miracle occurred on the drive to the new program that changed them from difficult, drug-affected, "problem" youth into "exceptional young people" who were not typical of the population, but that miracle had nothing to do with them. The miracle resulted from the fact that the staff and Board at the new program didn't meet them as difficult, drug-affected, "problem" youth -- they met them as *paid youth consultants* who were there to evaluate the program and offer suggestions for improvement. This pre-disposed the staff to an entirely different set of beliefs and expectations about the young people, and they saw in the young people what they *expected* to see.

To successfully implement a Youth Development approach and build Protective Factors that foster a young person's innate capacity for resiliency, the first and most challenging barrier to overcome is the one created by our own beliefs and expectations. A difficult part of this challenge is that we live in a culture that plays many "tapes" about young people, and most of these tapes are recordings of negative assumptions (young people are lazy, impulsive, dangerous, self-centered). These tapes and negative assumptions create dismissive beliefs and low expectations. Even if you consider yourself an advocate for young people, it takes effort and intention to overcome these tapes and communicate High Expectations. The following exercise is designed to illuminate this challenge.

STOP **Make a commitment** ... Pick a period of time (e.g., for the next week) or a specific activity (e.g., for the next 4 staff meetings) or a specific environment (e.g., when I'm at school) and pay attention to the *descriptors*, that is, any word or phrase that defines or qualifies young people or young people's behaviors/actions, that are being used when young people are discussed. Write them down and keep a log below (you may simply place a hash mark next to a descriptor that is used more than once). <u>Do not tell anyone what you are doing</u>. When finished, categorize the descriptors in terms of positive or negative by circling (+) or (-), and compare the ratio. You may continue with this lesson before completing this task, but make a commitment to follow-through.

_____ (+) (-) _____ (+) (-) _____ (+) (-)

_____ (+) (-) _____ (+) (-) _____ (+) (-)

_____ (+) (-) _____ (+) (-) _____ (+) (-)

_____ (+) (-) _____ (+) (-) _____ (+) (-)

_____ (+) (-) _____ (+) (-) _____ (+) (-)

_____ (+) (-) _____ (+) (-) _____ (+) (-)

_____ (+) (-) _____ (+) (-) _____ (+) (-)

_____ (+) (-) _____ (+) (-) _____ (+) (-)

GO When I conducted this activity at a weekly meeting of street-dependent youth case managers, negative descriptors outnumbered positive descriptors 9-1, and I discovered something else that was notable. The descriptor "manipulative" was utilized more than any other single descriptor. Yet when I viewed the context, it was always a youth going to an agency or staff person and not getting what they wanted *from their perspective*. Certainly there can be debate about the validity of their perspective or what it was that they were wanting, but never-the-less they weren't getting it so they went to another agency or staff person and tried again. It was then that I realized that this was a behavior that I engage in *all of the time*. If I don't like the way my hair is cut, I go to a different barber. If I don't like the way a doctor treats me, I go to a different doctor. Nobody calls me *manipulative*. They call me *resourceful*.

The fact is, almost any human behavior or action can be viewed in the negative or in the positive. The question is; on which viewpoint do you focus? This question becomes even more critical when you realize that you will inevitably get more of *that on which you focus*.

I challenge you to raise your awareness of your own language and the language of those around you when it comes to descriptors applied to young people. Our language shapes our thoughts, our thoughts shape our beliefs and expectations, and our beliefs and expectations shape the cues that we send to the young people with whom we interact. To change *their* behavior we must first change *our* beliefs and expectations. The Pygmalion Effect will create conformity with the beliefs and expectations that we hold, so the first step in creating Protective Factor environments is to assure that we hold beliefs and expectations that represent the best in young people. "Red Flags," in Appendix C, is a self-assessment tool that may be used to assist you in this area.

The Challenge of Pygmalion

While most people can get behind the Pygmalion Effect in theory, the challenge is in its practice. The fact that people will conform to other's beliefs and expectations indicates that they may not fit those beliefs and expectations prior to their conformation. This is not that big of a challenge in most areas where you see PYD applied, as a simple internet search will confirm that PYD is mostly presented in the context of mainstream youth organizations such as sports programs, 4-H, and similar venues, where a majority of the youth may already have many Protective Factors in their lives, and few or mild Risk Factors. In these programs, it may be easy to see and believe the best in young people, as they may already be on a path of healthy development and exhibiting positive behaviors. But as PYD is increasingly applied to high-risk populations such as runaway and street dependent youth, drug-affected youth, youth in the juvenile justice system, youth who may be failing in the education system, and other marginalized youth populations, the challenge of Pygmalion becomes more pronounced. In fact, a tragedy of the youth work field is seeing people go into the field believing the best in young people, and over time *conforming to the young people's beliefs about themselves* -- sort of a reverse Pygmalion. It can be both challenging and difficult to treat people as valuable, competent, and capable when they are doing everything in their power to prove to you what a worthless piece of crap they are (as they may believe themselves to be). But that is the challenge of working with high-risk populations; to see in them what they don't see in themselves. This is why High Expectations cannot be "faked" -- you actually have to *believe* that the young people with whom you are interacting are, at their core, good, competent, and capable. That may not be how they're acting right now, but that's *who* they are. You act towards them according to *your* belief, not according to *their* behavior. Your belief in them has to be stronger than their disbelief in themselves.

Summation

- We interact with people offering various conscious and unconscious cues as to our beliefs and expectations. People receiving these cues adjust their behavior to match the cues they are receiving. This is known as the Pygmalion Effect.
- Many beliefs and expectations related to young people are negative. To foster resiliency and promote development, we must overcome these negative beliefs and expectations and communicate positive beliefs and messages (High Expectations). This cannot be faked ... you actually have to *have* High Expectations of young people; it is something that you need to *believe*.

Learning Assignment 4
Complete **BEFORE** proceeding

Part 1a: Jointly engage one or more adults AND one or more young people (19 or younger) in a discussion about adult and societal attitudes toward young people (You may use your youth and adult learning partners, or a new group of young people and adults; be prepared to explain your terminology if needed). Pay attention to the way in which the adult(s) and young person(s) respond. After the discussion, answer the questions on the next page.

1. How are the responses similar?

_____

_____

_____

2. How are the responses different?

_____

_____

_____

3. How would you characterize adult and societal attitudes toward young people?

_____

_____

_____

4. How would you characterize young people's perceptions of adult and societal attitudes?

_____

_____

_____

Part 1b: In preparation for the next lesson, think about and write answers for the following four questions:

1. What does "youth participation" mean to you?

_____

_____

_____

2. Why do you want young people to participate?

_____

_____

_____

3. What does youth participation look like?

_____

_____

_____

4. What are the benefits of youth participation?

_____

_____

_____

Part 2: <u>After</u> completing Parts 1a and 1b, meet with your supervisor (or adult learning partner) and discuss the questions on the next page. Write down the key points of your discussion.

1. What did you learn from Lesson 4 and/or your interview(s) that was new for you?

_____

_____

_____

2. What did you re-learn or remember as a result of Lesson 4 and/or your interview(s)?

_____

_____

_____

3. List the key thoughts, points, or ideas that you want to remember from Lesson 4 and/or your interview(s). You may list as many items as you wish, but list at least 3.

_____

_____

_____

GO If you have completed Parts 1a, 1b, and 2 of Learning Assignment 4, you may now move on to Lesson 5.

Lesson 5
Meaningful Participation

Tell me, I'll forget. Show me, I may remember. But involve me, and I'll understand.

~ Attributed to many sources, but most likely a Chinese proverb ~

In this lesson you will learn:

- Lesson Anchor: Jack of Diamonds
- Purpose of Participation
- Theory of Participation
- Forms of Participation
- Strategies for Participation

Lesson Anchor: Jack of Diamonds

The fourth card in your Winning Hand is the **Jack of Diamonds**. Please draw it now and place it with your Ace of Hearts from Lesson 2, your Eight of Spades from Lesson 3, and your Joker from Lesson 4, which should be a location where you see it often. This is the anchor card for **Lesson 5 - - Meaningful Participation**.

The message of Lesson 4 was that we will get out of young people what we see in them, so it is critical that we *maximize* our attention to their strengths and abilities and *minimize* our attention to their deficits and challenges. Your ability to see and focus on the positive in young people is a necessary prerequisite to successfully engaging them as meaningful participants. A student will not learn unless he believes that his teacher believes that he *can* learn. A player will not play unless she believes that her coach believes that she *can* play. Young people will not participate unless they believe that others believe that they have something to contribute. Seeing the best in young people, especially when they do not yet see it in themselves, is the *minimum standard* to which we must adhere if we wish to involve youth as partners and participants. This is why the Jack is the anchor for this lesson, as the Jack is often used to represent a *minimum standard* (you poker players know that you have to have at least *Jacks or better* to open). And, just as the suit of spades was used idiomatically to remind us to utilize the (s)OS framework *a lot*, the suit of diamonds was also selected for an idiomatic usage of the term. You've heard of a *diamond in the rough*. When used like this, *diamond in the rough* means *having exceptionally good qualities or the potential for greatness, but lacking polish or refinement*. This is an apt description of young people when they are first given opportunities to participate. They may lack "polish or refinement" as such things come with experience, but they have exceptionally good qualities and the potential for greatness if we are patient enough to allow them to *gain* experience. We will see both the "diamond" and the "rough," but it is the diamond upon which we must focus.

As you begin this lesson, remember that the **Ace of Hearts** reminds you that outcomes are the "Bottom Line" of youth work, and you know in your heart what young people need to develop into healthy and successful adolescents and adults (DO's, or Developmental Outcomes.). The **Eight of Spades** reminds you that the framework for the Youth Development approach, is to *minimize* services (*to* or *for*) and to *maximize* Opportunities and Supports (*by* and *with*) which should be applied *to a considerable degree, without end* (*in spades* for *infinity*). The **Joker** reminds us that young people will conform to our beliefs and expectations about them, so our "highest trump" is to believe the best about young people, even and especially when they don't believe the best about themselves (the Pygmalion Effect). Now, to continue to build Protective Factors into the (s)OS framework that will foster resiliency, take the information presented in this lesson and remember that the *minimum standard* for successful participation is your focus on young people's *exceptionally good qualities and their potential for greatness*.

Purpose of Participation

Before discussing *how* to create meaningful participation, it is worth reviewing *why* we wish to do so, and to consider some theory underpinning participation strategies.

Youth Development as a practice is about creating Protective Factor environments that foster young people's innate capacity for resiliency. This is why we use (s)OS as the framework for implementing PYD. By creating Opportunities and providing Supports, that is, things that are done *by* young people *with* adult guidance and support, we create a context for High

Expectations (the first of the Protective Factors). But things can't be done by young people, which as earlier defined is necessarily an act of *volition*, unless young people are active participants in the opportunity. Thus the second Protective Factor, Meaningful Participation, is also integral to the (s)OS framework.

It needs to be clarified, however, that youth participation is not in and of itself Youth Development; it is a *component* of Youth Development. Misunderstanding the relationship of youth participation to Youth Development can result in misapplication of the theory. For example, programs may claim to be Youth Development programs because they have young people on their Board of Directors or they maintain a Youth Advisory Board. While both of these are excellent strategies of participation, they may not represent a program based on PYD.

What is often misinterpreted as the goal of youth participation is the value of giving young people a voice in services and programs, and the benefits to services and programs from including that voice. This is why when you see youth participation in action it so often takes the form of some kind of group or "Board" that includes young people in a consultation or influence role[12]. However, these benefits, which are real, are a *consequence* of youth participation, not the *goal*. We seek to create opportunities for young people to participate because Meaningful Participation is one of the three Protective Factors that fosters resiliency.

Understanding why we seek young people's participation begs the question; which young people do we wish to see participate? The answer, of course, is *all* of them. If Meaningful Participation is a Protective Factor that fosters resiliency, each and every young person needs to participate meaningfully. Seats on Boards of Directors or Youth Advisory Councils are excellent opportunities, but only for the relatively small number of young people that such opportunities can accommodate. What about everyone else?

This is not to advocate against such strategies. Rather, it is to point out the necessity to have a range and depth of strategies that ensures that all young people have the opportunity to experience meaningful participation, as the purpose is not what participation does for *us*, but rather what participation does for *young people*.

Theory of Participation

Simply stated, the Youth Development theory related to participation is that all young people can and will participate. If young people are not participating the problem is not with the young person, the problem is with the opportunity.

To ensure participation, an opportunity must meet three standards. Failure to meet even one of these standards will inhibit participation. As many people have some familiarity with a Youth Advisory Council as a strategy for participation, we'll use that in our examples.

Standard 1: Clarity -- The Opportunity must be Clear

By "clear" we mean that the opportunity must be easily understood, without ambiguity, entirely comprehensible, free from confusion and completely evident. All of this, of course, is in reference to the young person whose participation you desire. Participation is not motivated by things being clear to *you*, but by things being clear to the *young person*.

Creating clarity involves a multitude of considerations. Communication and language, developmental levels, and cultural and environmental context, all play a role in whether or not an opportunity is clearly understood. Structure and purpose, however, also play enormous roles, and are often the least clear aspects of an opportunity.

This is the case with many Youth Advisory Councils. They may be formed based on a belief that having a Youth Advisory Council is a good idea, but the purpose, charge, and authority of the Council, or even the manner in which the Council is structured or functions, may be either under-developed or confusing. If this is the case, you can expect the Council to under-perform or fail completely, and getting young people's commitment to participate will be challenging.

Standard 2: Legitimacy -- The Opportunity must be Legitimate

By "legitimate" we mean that, whatever the opportunity purports to offer, it must fully and genuinely offer. It must not hold out the promise of things that will not be gained, nor falsely represent the benefits of participation.

This is closely related to being clear, as legitimacy is judged by its relationship to clarity. Using our Youth Advisory Council example again, a case of illegitimacy might occur if the Council is lead to believe that they have authority that in practice they do not possess. For example, a Youth Council is told that they have authority over rule development, but then they develop rules that program administration does not like and disallows. If the Council did not know in advance that their decisions could be negated by higher authority, the legitimacy of the opportunity suffers.

To ensure legitimacy, avoid embellishing the benefits and responsibilities of participation efforts. If an accurate, honest appraisal of an opportunity's attractions fails to motivate participation, then it *should* fail. Effort should be focused on changing the opportunity rather than on how the opportunity is marketed.

Standard 3: Relevancy -- The Opportunity must be Relevant

The first question to ask is; relevant to *whom?* The answer obviously is; relevant to the young person that you wish to see participate. But this answer alone does not get to the heart of the matter. The real question is; relevant in whose *judgment?* The answer doesn't change, but it does put a new spin on our perspective.

One of the biggest contributors to young people failing to participate, and therefore confirming a belief that they are unwilling to participate, is that opportunities are often what *adults* decide is relevant. We can make all kinds of philosophical arguments that a particular opportunity is relevant to a young person's health, or needs, or growth, or development. We may even be right, in the "big picture" sense. None of that matters if the individual young person does not see the opportunity as relevant to them based on what *they* believe and feel and see for themselves *right now*. If they need to be convinced that an opportunity is relevant to them, *it isn't*.

One of the best ways to ensure relevancy is to include young people in the creation of the opportunity. A group of adults is simply not going to create opportunities that are as relevant to young people as those that they have a part in creating. Another barrier is created when we forget that relevance is a standard that is in constant change, and this state of change is affected by both individuality and time.

Relevance is an individual determinant. One young person or group of young people cannot create relevance for others. It is a common mistake for adults to assume that *any* young person can represent *all* young people -- which is as false as believing that any adult can represent all adults. As participation in an opportunity changes or expands, relevance may be affected. Even if the actual participants don't change, time is another impacting factor. What is relevant in the winter may not be relevant in the summer. The adolescent relationship to time[13], particularly in its present-focus, means that what is relevant *today* may not be relevant *tomorrow*. This is another strong argument in favor of partnering with participants in the creation and evolution of opportunities. The more young people are involved in how the opportunity develops, the more relevant to *them* the opportunity will remain.

If an opportunity is clear, legitimate, and relevant -- and you avoid the trap of thinking that early success with an opportunity means continued success without change (or early failure means the opportunity will *never* work) -- you will be rewarded with active participation by young people. Fail in any one of these three areas, and you will be disappointed with the level of participation.

Forms of Participation

When creating opportunities for meaningful participation, it is helpful to think in terms of *forms* and *strategies*. "Strategies" refers to intentional structures built into the environment that give young people "avenues" of participation. They are structures that by design encourage, promote, or necessitate participation. But, as a Protective Factor, participation should be *the environment*, not just the structure. It should be the basis of and standard for most if not all interaction; even small daily encounters that may not be a part of a structured strategy. To meet this goal it is helpful to think in terms of *forms* that participation may take. While not an exhaustive list, the 5 forms that follow represent the most common ways to create an environment of participation.

Choosing: This is perhaps the simplest and most common form of youth participation, as well as the form most applicable to very young children. It involves clarifying a set of options, any of which is an acceptable option to pursue. Which one of the options is pursued is left up to the participation of youth. It is critical that youth are able to make informed choices, however, so any participation involving choice should also involve education about the choices. This education should include an unbiased presentation of pros and cons, as well as reasons for boundaries (why these are the only choices, for example).

Decision-making: This differs from choosing in that there are no pre-determined options. Instead, the option is created in response to defined conditions, problems, or circumstances. When young people are involved in decision making, they are not necessarily solely responsible for the decision. It is preferable that they are *included as* decision-makers rather than *designated as* decision-makers. Think in terms of partnership rather than delegation. Don't just give them a decision to make, but rather include them as part of and contributors to a decision made in partnership with adults.

Assessing or Evaluating: This involves a range of activities, from simple feedback to formal evaluative processes. It does not necessarily include change, that is, the act of giving feedback or evaluating from the young person's perspective does not have to be more than advice for those in authority to consider. However, it does not preclude direct impact, either. Incorporating youth feedback as a formal part of staff evaluation (for example) could be implemented with either emphasis. The feedback could be utilized simply to make staff aware of how young people are viewing their performance, or the youth's feedback could directly affect the outcome of a staff's performance appraisal. These two different approaches are applicable to any form of youth assessment or evaluation.

Planning: This form is similar to decision-making as it is often preferable that planning be considered as a partnership between young people and adults. In this regard, planning is an appropriate form of participation for everything from how to use an hour of free time, to how to manage and operate a program or service, to how to develop a proposal for funding. The distinguishing characteristic of planning is the development of a means to an end. What that end is may result from choosing or decision-making, but how to reach that end is the result of planning.

Communicating: This refers to any form of youth participation where the young person communicates information, either in writing or through speaking. It can take the form of information and referral, tours and orientations, media contact, grant writing, artistic expression, and public speaking, just to name a few possible scenarios. While this is one of the more powerful forms of youth participation in terms of associated benefits, it comes with a caution.

Communicating is often the earliest form of youth participation that programs embrace. This is a result of the fact that youth presenting a case or speaking on behalf of a program has proved to be a powerful means of reaching the public, stake holders, and policy makers. Programs are often comfortable letting young people be spokespersons long before they are comfortable letting them be decision-makers and, in fact, youth are often actively encouraged to accept these roles. The caution here is that almost every study of human fears and phobias ranks public speaking as the thing we fear the *most*, consistently coming in greater than the fear of *death*. Considering that, we need to be careful about the pressure we put on young people to speak in public. There are many youth who may be comfortable and articulate in front of strangers, but there are also many who would rather die than stand up in front of a group. For every youth keynote I've seen where the young person was fabulous, I've seen another young person who was frozen. Communicating is a form of youth participation that should be used judiciously and offered only to youth who have demonstrated interest and comfort.

Strategies of Participation

At several points in this workbook I've talked about how Positive Youth Development is a new and evolving field, creating lack of consensus in how concepts are presented. Strategies for youth participation are not immune to this condition and your research beyond this workbook will discover ways of discussing this topic that are different from how it is presented here. Like Developmental Outcomes and Protective Factors, the important thing is the *concept*, not the specific presentation, so you should feel free to use what makes sense to you and works in your setting.

Most sources present strategies for participation as a spectrum, scale, or ladder, ranging from "less" participation to "more" participation. The presentation in this workbook uses a similar format and is a compilation of various sources[14].

 Before you proceed ... turn to Appendix D and review *A Spectrum of Youth Participation -- An Evolutionary View*. This is a content resource, not an exercise.

 Refer to this resource as you continue with this lesson.

The first thing to be aware of is that this paradigm suggests that the creation of successful youth participation is an *evolutionary* process. In other words, success with "higher" strategies is related to success with the preceding strategy, and each strategy will naturally tend to *evolve* to the next level. For example, a strategy of *Influence* will be more successful if *Consultation* has already been implemented, and successful *Influence* will naturally tend to evolve to strategies of *Partnership*. Therefore, the ideal method of implementation is to begin with Ad Hoc[15] Input and, when that is well institutionalized, then proceed to Consultation.

Listing these strategies as separate structures and suggesting that you start with one and evolve to others is not meant to imply that these strategies should be implemented as single or isolated efforts. Meaningful Participation is a Protective Factor that all youth need to have in their environment. To accomplish this goal, these strategies may need to have multiple implementations over the full spectrum, depending upon the requirements of the setting in which you are working with young people. In other words, the ideal would be to make Ad Hoc Input the standard operating procedure within your environment, and multiple Consultation, Influence, and Partnership opportunities would exist to ensure that _all young people_ have the opportunity to be involved as appropriate to their developmental level and their level of interest (relevancy).

This evolutionary view provides an overview of each strategy in the spectrum. Included are the concept and implications of the strategy, a few _brief_ ideas for implementation, as well as some of the advantages and disadvantages inherent in each. Additionally it details how each different "level" in the spectrum relates to issues of time commitment, impact on developmental outcomes, level of participation, and numbers able to participate. Note that in the former 3 areas, the spectrum moves from less to greater, meaning that strategies at the "higher" end of the spectrum will require greater time commitment in terms of adult support, have more significant impact on developmental outcomes, and require more of each participant in terms of their individual effort and commitment. Only the latter area -- the _number_ of participants -- moves from _greater_ to _smaller_, meaning that higher-end strategies accommodate decreased numbers of young people. While all young people can experience Ad Hoc Input strategies, only a few young people can experience a specific partnership strategy. To compensate for this in environments with large numbers of young people, higher-end strategies may need to be multiple and/or duplicated.

But it's Just Me

Obviously, most of the information in this lesson is written to be applicable to an agency, classroom, program, or on-going group setting. Some of you reading this, however, may be alone in your efforts to implement a PYD approach, either because you are not operating in an environment that has made a commitment to PYD, or because you are interacting with youth in some form of one-to-one situation (e.g., therapist; Big Brother or Sister, Tutor). If you think in terms of _partnering_ with the young person you'll discover that these forms and strategies of participation are not only applicable to on-going group situations, but also to one-time individual encounters. The cognitive leap you need to make is that, regardless of the relationship, the young person is your _partner_. A therapist is not trying to _fix her client_, she is _partnering with her client_ to resolve identified issues. A Big Brother is not trying to be an _adult mentor to a child_, he is _partnering with the child_ to create a significant youth/adult relationship. A tutor is not trying to *educate her student*, she is *partnering with her student* to address educational needs. If you are able to view your relationship through the lens of *partnership* you will discover daily opportunities to utilize the forms and strategies of participation described in this lesson.

Summation

- Youth participation is a component of the Youth Development approach. To be effective, it must be used as a Protective Factor within the PYD framework.

- Youth participation is one of the three Protective Factors that fosters the innate capacity for resiliency. While consumer input benefits the program or service, that is not its goal or purpose. It is the benefit to the young person that is the reason for youth participation, and therefore strategies must be employed that allow all young people to participate appropriate to their level of development.

- All young people can and will participate if the opportunity is clear, legitimate, and relevant. If young people are not participating the problem is not with the young person, the problem is with the opportunity.

- Youth participation takes five main forms; Choosing, Decision Making, Assessing or Evaluating, Planning, and Communicating. Care should be taken with Communicating, as some people find it extremely uncomfortable.

- The four primary strategies for youth participation are Ad Hoc Input, Consultation, Influence, and Partnership.

 Learning Assignment 5
Complete **BEFORE** proceeding

Part 1a: It should be apparent after reading Lesson 5 that the Learning Assignments you've been completing with your youth learning partners have involved various forms and strategies of Meaningful Participation, even though they were not discussed until this lesson. Reflect upon your experience with the previous Learning Assignments, and answer the questions on the next page.

1. What *forms* of participation have you used in the previous Learning Assignments?

_____

_____

_____

2. What *strategies* of participation have you used in the previous Learning Assignments?

_____

_____

_____

3. What would you have done differently based on the information contained in Lesson 5?

_____

_____

_____

Part 1b: Interview your youth learning partner(s) and discuss their experience of your efforts to include them as Meaningful Participants. Specifically seek feedback on how you could have improved their participation. Record their ideas below:

_____

_____

_____

_____

_____

Part 2: <u>After</u> completing Parts 1a and 1b, meet with your supervisor (or adult learning partner) and discuss the following questions. Write the key points of your discussion below:

1. What did you learn from Lesson 5 and/or your interview(s) that was new for you?

_____

_____

_____

2. What did you re-learn or remember as a result of Lesson 5 and/or your interview(s)?

_____

_____

_____

3. List the key thoughts, points, or ideas that you want to remember from Lesson 5 and/or your interview(s). You may list as many items as you wish, but list at least <u>3</u>.

_____

_____

_____

GO <u>If you have completed Parts 1a, 1b, and 2 of Learning Assignment 5</u>, you may now move on to Lesson 6.

Lesson 6
Caring, Supportive Relationships

I've learned that people will forget what you said, people will forget what you did, but people will never forget how you made them feel.

~ Maya Angelou ~

In this lesson you will learn:

- Lesson Anchor: Queen of Clubs
- What are "Core Competencies"
- Youth Development Basic Skills

Lesson Anchor: Queen of Clubs

The final card in your Winning Hand is the **Queen of Clubs**. Please draw it now and place it with your Ace of Hearts from Lesson 2, your Eight of Spades from Lesson 3, your Joker from Lesson 4, and your Jack of Diamonds from Lesson 5, which should be a location where you see it often. This is the anchor card for **Lesson 6 -- Caring, Supportive Relationships**.

The Queen was selected to represent the natural female tendency to relate, as opposed to the male tendency toward the analytical. The reason why your Winning Hand uses the Queen of *Clubs* has to do with a specific definition of "club." In one meaning, to "club" means to *unite, combine,* to *join together.* This describes one of the foundational assumptions of the Youth Development approach; that we are working *with* young people instead of *to* or *for* them. The definition also describes the relationship we want with our colleagues and other adults; that we are joining together to create Protective Factor environments for young people. Supporting this unity of effort requires self-examination; what are the core competencies demanded by a Youth Development approach, and to what degree do I possess these competencies? The message of the Queen of Clubs is to unite through *relationship* as a means for creating Protective Factor environments, and developing our personal core competencies is the means to that end.

As you begin this lesson, remember that the **Ace of Hearts** reminds you that outcomes are the "Bottom Line" of youth work, and you know in your heart what young people need to develop into healthy and successful adolescents and adults (DO's, or Developmental Outcomes.). The **Eight of Spades** reminds you that the framework for the Youth Development approach, is to *minimize* services (*to* or *for*) and to *maximize* Opportunities and Supports (*by* and *with*) which should be applied *to a considerable degree, without end* (*in spades* for *infinity*). The **Joker** reminds us that young people will conform to our beliefs and expectations about them, so our "highest trump" is to believe the best about young people, even and especially when they don't believe the best about themselves (the Pygmalion Effect). The **Jack of Diamonds** reminds us that the *minimum standard* for successful participation is your focus on young people's *exceptionally good qualities and their potential for greatness* (through forms and strategies for Meaningful Participation, and ensuring that opportunities are clear, legitimate, and relevant). Now, to continue to build Protective Factors into the (s)OS framework that will foster resiliency, take the information presented in this lesson and remember that Caring, Supportive Relationships are created based on our personal skills and competencies.

What are "Core Competencies"

To be "competent" means to have "*suitable or sufficient skill, knowledge, experience, etc., for some purpose; properly qualified*" and to *have* a competency means that you are skilled or qualified to do something. However, a competency refers to something that is specific rather than general. For example, you may be qualified to be a pilot -- you may even be considered to be a competent pilot -- but there is no such thing as a *single* pilot competency. Rather, being a pilot requires a *range* of competencies (e.g., ground procedures, flight maneuvers, navigation) which, when all are mastered, qualify you as a pilot.

Any field of endeavor will require mastery in a lengthy list of competencies to excel at that endeavor. But the concept of "competent" does not refer to *excelling*, it refers to *adequate*, "properly qualified." This is where we discover the concept of "core" competencies.

Core Competencies originally developed as a management concept referring to the central functions or operations of a business. A specific business may do a lot of things, but there are only a few things that are central and essential to the growth and success of the company. To survive in a competitive environment, a business needs to prioritize its core competencies over any other competencies that it may possess.

This concept expanded to individual performance within occupations. To succeed in a profession one needs to master many competencies, but each profession has a specific set of "core" competencies that are essential to adequate performance. The idea is that you may master many competencies, but if you fail to master the "core" competencies required by your job you won't be very successful. Mastering the many competencies that may benefit your performance beyond the core competencies will help you to excel in your profession, but if you haven't mastered the "core" competencies, you cannot adequately do your job, no matter how good you are at additional competencies.

Different resources list different numbers of core competencies that a profession may require, but the number is almost always in the 5 to 9 range[16]. Sometimes it goes up a little higher, and I've even seen lists that include dozens of competencies. These longer lists generally have moved beyond the concept of a "core" set and are now focusing on all of the competencies a position may require. Most resources focused on core competencies discuss a small and specific set.

Within the field of Youth Development there has been much attention to defining core competency sets. The resulting different lists may be seen as yet another manifestation of PYD's continuing evolution, similar to the different presentations of Developmental Outcomes, Strategies for Participation, and other PYD concepts. However, they differ in one significant way; they can be radically dissimilar and even contradictory of each other. The result is that core competencies is probably the least developed concept within the Youth Development approach.

I have a theory on this, and my presentation of core competencies is grounded in this theory. It is based on something we learned way back in Lesson 1. In that lesson, when we defined Youth Development, we learned that it is an *approach*, not a *model*. PYD is not *what* you do, but rather it is the *way* that you do it. Given that, it should be self-evident why there is no agreement on Youth Development core competencies, because competencies reference *what* you do, they do not speak to *how* you do it.

This is not to say that your job will not have a defined set of core competencies. Rather it is to say that the set of core competencies you will need to implement Youth Development in your position will differ depending on what your position is. The core competencies needed to adequately perform as a state case worker implementing PYD will be different from the core competencies needed to adequately perform as a street outreach worker implementing PYD, which will also be different from the core competencies needed to adequately perform as a teacher implementing PYD, and so on. In light of this, mastering the Youth Development approach requires development of a *basic skill set* that enables you to work in partnership with young people in a manner that promotes High Expectations, Meaningful Participation, and Caring, Supportive Relationships. This lesson focuses on those basic skills, but you are encouraged to additionally define and master the specific core competencies needed to adequately perform within your position.

 Before you proceed ... turn to Appendix D and refer to the chart A Spectrum of Youth Participation -- An Evolutionary View. This is a content resource, not an exercise.

 Refer to this resource as you continue with this lesson.

Youth Development Basic Skills

The goal is to foster young people's innate capacity for resiliency by creating Protective Factor environments consisting of High Expectations, Meaningful Participation, and Caring, Supportive Relationships. The framework we use to do this is to create Opportunities and provide Supports. In utilizing this framework, we interact with young people as partners and implement strategies that engage young people as participants. Therefore, the success of our Youth Development efforts, regardless of the model in which they are applied, ultimately rests on our success with implementing strategies of participation. So, when I speak of Youth Development basic skills, I'm referring to the skills required to be successful with those strategies. In Lesson 5 we discussed 4 specific strategies; Ad Hoc Input, Consultation, Influence, and Partnership. In this lesson we'll look at the basic skills required to be successful with these strategies. As with the concept of core competencies, I am not implying that these are the only skills you will need to master, but if you don't master at least these 4 skills, implementation of the PYD strategies will suffer.

Basic Skill for Ad Hoc Input

The strategy of Ad Hoc Input involves seeking, hearing, respecting, valuing, and considering the views and concerns of young people. It is about creating an environment where young people act as *contributors to*, rather than *recipients of*. An additional implied requirement is that young people feel sought, heard, respected, valued, and considered. Essential to all of this is one basic skill; Attentive Listening[17].

Attentive Listening is actually a *set* of skills for hearing and responding to another person. By employing these skills, communication is enhanced and mutual understanding is promoted. It is not only essential to promoting participation by young people, but it is one of the primary ways that the "caring" part of Caring, Supportive Relationships is perceived by young people. Unfortunately, Attentive Listening is such a common concept within the helping profession that most people do not use it effectively, particularly in youth/adult relationships. Adults are often much better at attentive *guiding*, attentive *teaching*, and attentive *lecturing* than we are at Attentive *Listening*. The skill more often than not is something of which adults are aware, but do not utilize as much as they could.

If you haven't attended Attentive Listening training, read some resources on Attentive Listening, or intentionally role played and practiced Attentive Listening skills within the past 6 months, you are probably not benefiting from the full potential of Attentive Listening when you interact with young people. In order to successfully implement the strategy of Ad Hoc Input, and create an environment where young people feel cared about and supported, the obtainment, practice, and application of formal Attentive Listening skills needs to be a priority in your professional development.

 Before you proceed ... turn to Appendix E and find the chart Guidelines for Attentive Listening and Reflection. This is a content resource, not an exercise.

 Refer to this resource as you continue with this lesson.

These Guidelines for Attentive Listening and Reflection provide a brief overview of some of the Attentive Listening skills required to promote Ad Hoc Input. This is only a review of a general approach to Attentive Listening, however. You are strongly encouraged to pursue further training and other resources. Program leaders and supervisors are encouraged to make the practice of Attentive Listening skills and on-going part of training and staff professional development.

 Engage a young person in conversation (19 or younger. It may be a youth learning partners, a youth with whom you are working, or any other youth). Practice Attentive Listening as follows:

Restrict your end of the conversation to only 3 responses.

1. Identifying/Acknowledging Feelings:

   - *It sounds like that made you angry.*
   - *I can see that you felt very competent doing that.*

2. Requesting Greater Detail or Clarification

   - *Can you say more about that?*
   - *Was anyone else involved?*

3. Restating to Assure Understanding:

   - *You're saying that the lesson is too advanced for you.*
   - *So you don't mind vegetables, as long as they're cooked.*

Note: Do not evaluate or judge what they are saying. Simply rephrase it to assure that you *comprehend* what they are saying.

After practicing this exercise, record your answers to the following questions:

1. What was this experience like for you?

_____

_____

_____

2. What if any difference did you notice in the young person's communication based on your Attentive Listening?

_____

_____

_____

 When you have completed this assignment you may continue with this lesson.

Basic Skill for Consultation

The strategy of Consultation involves deliberate structures to seek young people's opinions about specific needs, targeted issues, or responses to identified situations. It is about creating an environment of *"we"* as opposed to one of *"us/them."* An additional implied requirement is that young people are acting from a place of *informed* participation. Essential to all of this is one basic skill; Information Sharing.

Adults are not accustomed to sharing information with young people. The inner workings of a program and the outside and internal pressures that adult staff deals with on a daily basis are often treated as arcane knowledge that we protect young people from the burden of having to know. We need to get over this and learn to be comfortable sharing information with young people if we wish to see successful Consultation efforts. Consider the following real life example.

I was asked to sit in on an initial meeting of a Youth Advisory Board at a drop in/shelter for street-dependent youth. Staff opened the meeting with the following statement:

> *"We've called this meeting to hear your ideas. After all, this is your program and it can be anything you want it to be, so what would you like to see happen?"*

Without hesitation, ideas began to flow. The first was a suggestion that the program establish *Drug Abuse Friday*, allowing the young people to come to the program under the influence that day. This was followed in rapid succession by equally unhelpful ideas.

Suggestion after suggestion was rejected, due to the fact that they were all as silly and unworkable as was *Drug Abuse Friday*. Eventually, the young people stopped making suggestions and the meeting ended, at which time I met with a staff who was scratching their heads wondering what went wrong.

There were two specific things that occurred that contributed to the failure of this Consultation strategy. The first was the dynamic that was created by staff consistently shooting down the young people's ideas. Every time a suggestion was made it was responded to with *no, we can't do that*. Of course, this wasn't the staff's fault; the ideas were not *doable*. Never-the-less, how often do you have to hear *no* before you stop contributing?

My second point, however, is what was responsible for setting up that dynamic, and this is something over which staff *did* have control. They began the meeting by *lying* to the young people. Remember, they said *this is your program and it can be anything you want it to be* (I wrote that line down, so I know that it is an exact quote). But here's the truth: No it's not, and no it can't. It is a publicly funded program with a specific mandate for the provision of defined services. There are funding limitations, legal requirements, standards of care, and outcome measurements, to name just a few of the internal and external factors that govern what the program can or can't do, and how it can operate. None of this information was provided to the young people.

The meeting should have started with sharing this information. Only after the participants understood the parameters within which decisions needed to be made could they realistically be expected to contribute something of value. Had this been done, *Drug Abuse Friday* suggestions would not have been made, as the participants would already be aware that such an event was not possible.

But, realistically, there is often information that cannot be shared. Employment laws, confidentiality, and other such information-restricting influences sometimes prevent the free-flow of information. However, every piece of information that cannot be shared has a *reason* why it can't be shared. In these cases, what you can do is *share the reason*. Getting in the habit of sharing reasons overcomes one of the greatest challenges to youth/adult communication, which is how to get past the favorite question of all young people ... "why?" By sharing the reason, you answer that question, and you will find that most young people are more than willing to accept even things with which they disagree if you have honestly answered that question.

As an example, I operated a self-government[18] structured youth shelter during a time when the city passed an anti-smoking ordinance in all public buildings. The shelter at the time permitted smoking in restricted areas, but had to go smoke-free when the ordinance was passed, as we were considered a "public accommodation." Needless to say, there was much dissatisfaction with the new policy, and at every House Meeting (where the youth were involved as decision makers in the program's structure and operation) I could be assured that the smoking policy was going to be the first issue raised (this was a short-term shelter, so each House Meeting generally had new participants who were not at the previous House Meeting). I would bring a copy of the city ordinance to each meeting, listen to their disagreements with and suggestions for modifying the program policy (as though it were the first time I had heard them), and then ... after they had their chance to voice their concerns ... show them the ordinance which clarified that we were a public accommodation subject to the ordinance, which made it illegal for us to allow smoking. The response was always "oh," after which the issue was dropped and we'd move on to other business. Honestly sharing information, or sharing the reasons why information can't be shared (or something must or can't be done), is one of the most important skills to develop for the Youth Development approach.

Basic Skill for Influence

The strategy of Influence involves young people having a direct link to authority and at least a minimal impact on decisions. It is about creating an environment where young people have some level of *real bargaining power* that cannot be negated or circumvented. An additional implied requirement is that young people cannot be mandated to influence. Essential to all of this is one basic skill; Negotiation.

I should point out that this is often the "glass ceiling" of youth participation. Adults may be comfortable with strategies of Ad Hoc Input and Consultation because they essentially retain power and control with those strategies. With Influence, adults begin to *share* power and control, thus making this a much more challenging (threatening?) strategy. If young people are in a position where they have real bargaining power, such as a voting structure where each young person's vote influences decisions and outcomes, some of our traditional methods of interaction need to change. A traditional approach based on counseling, therapy, and/or advocacy is not useful in "bargaining" situations. Instead, these types of situations require negotiation skills.

Rarely in the youth service field are workers provided with negotiation training, putting the burden of learning negotiation techniques and skills squarely on the individual's shoulders. Fortunately, there are many resources including both printed/audio materials and live trainings/presentations that are available for you to acquire such skills, and a simple web search should get you started in the right direction. Be aware, however, that there are different styles of negotiation.

The two primary styles of negotiation are win/lose and win/win. In win/lose, two or more parties interact with each other having the goal of individually gaining the most while sacrificing the least. This style of negotiation is more or less a conflict oriented style and, as such, is not recommended for strategies of youth participation where working together in partnership is the outcome target. Instead, the skills that are appropriate to the strategy of influence are those inherent in the *win/win* style of negotiation. In this style the goal is for *all parties* to gain the most while sacrificing the least. For a comparison between win/lose and win/win, see Additional Information on Negotiation in Appendix F.

Basic Skill for Partnership

The strategy of Partnership involves young people acting with defined responsibilities for specific activities, tasks, or functions. It is about young people's involvement in the creation of, implementation of, and/or accountability for all or many of the important aspects of a defined area. An additional implied requirement is that young people have the responsibility for performing work and reaching goals. Essential to all of this is one basic skill; Delegation.

Delegation is a skill at which most people are not very good, mostly because it is misunderstood. It is often seen as "delegating" your problems, work, or responsibility to others. But delegation is not about assigning tasks or giving other people work to do. True delegation involves *entrusting authority*.

By way of example, let's say that your program is putting on a holiday celebration. The *ineffective* delegator will give you the job of making it happen, but retain all of the decision making authority. You will then have to constantly check in with them to make sure that you are doing it "right," resulting in more work than is necessary for you both. But an *effective* delegator will not only give you the task, they will give you the *authority*. They will tell you the outcome they want, the resources you have available to you, and any other information or guidelines necessary to create the outcome that they are seeking, and then say "see you at the celebration," leaving the authority to make the necessary decisions in your hands.

Delegation is not delegation unless it includes the *authority to react to situations and to make decisions*.

Three principles ensure effective delegation:

1. Those to whom you delegate know the desired outcome
2. Those to whom you delegate have the authority to act
3. Those to whom you delegate have available to them the knowledge, skills, ability, support, and resources necessary to achieve the desired outcome

In addition to these three principles, effective delegation depends on *clear communication* about:

1. The expected outcome(s)
2. The parameters and extent of discretionary authority
3. The sources of support, information, and knowledge that will be needed.

The cognitive shift that needs to be made when delegating, particularly when using this skill for the participation strategy of Partnership, is that you are not assigning *work*, you are delegating *authority*.

A Final Thought on Caring, Supportive Relationships

This lesson focused on Youth Development Basic Skills to be used in the context of specific strategies of participation, but it is important to not lose sight of the fact that the reason to practice these skills is to create and develop relationships that serve as Protective Factors. Refer back to the description of Caring, Supportive Relationships in Lesson 1 and you will see how these basic skills help shape a Protective Factor relationship. The *Caring* qualifier indicates that, *from the young person's perspective*, the relationship is based on genuine interest (promoted by Attentive Listening). The *Supportive* qualifier indicates that, *from the young person's perspective*, the relationship is seen as a viable resource (promoted by Information Sharing). Information Sharing also defines the relationship and establishes boundaries, which is further enhanced by *negotiation* and *delegation*. Anytime you interact with a young person a relationship is created. By adhering to these basic skills, and using them while demonstrating High Expectations and creating Opportunities and providing Supports as a way of assuring Meaningful Participation, the relationship will serve as a Protective Factor.

Summation

- The success of any endeavor is based on mastery of 5 to 9 "core competencies."
- There is a lack of consensus on the core competencies required for Positive Youth Development. This is probably because PYD is an *approach*, not a *model*.
- Mastery of 4 basic skills is required to create relationships that will serve as Protective Factors.
- The 4 basic skills are Attentive Listening (for Ad Hoc Input), Information Sharing (for Consultation), Win/Win Negotiating (for Influence), and Delegation (for Partnership).

 Review and Final Exam
Complete **BEFORE** proceeding

Congratulations! At this point you have completed all 6 lessons and have a basic working knowledge of the Youth Development Approach. Read through the chapter reviews that follow, and then demonstrate your knowledge by completing the Winning Hand Final Exam Crossword Puzzle. Upon correct completion of the puzzle you may take advantage of a special offer by completing the fisherman sentence (instructions follow the puzzle).

Lesson 1: An Introduction to the Positive Youth Development Approach

 There is a large body of research showing that all people have an innate capacity for resiliency, but external environmental factors affect that capacity. Risk Factors *inhibit* resiliency. Protective Factors (High Expectations, Meaningful Participation, and Caring and Supportive Relationships) *foster* resiliency. This became the foundation for a practice, or way of working with young people, that is known as the Youth Development approach, or Positive Youth Development, or PYD. As a concept Youth Development refers to a developmental *process* where young people seek ways to meet basic physical and social needs, and build competencies. As a practice Youth Development refers to an *approach* to working with young people that fosters their innate resiliency and supports their developmental process. Youth Development differs from Strength-based approaches in that it is developmental as opposed to problem focused.

75

Lesson 2: Youth Outcomes: The "Bottom Line" of Youth Work

 Outcomes, the "bottom line" of youth work, may be categorized as *achievement, prevention,* or *developmental.* Achievement outcomes are an increase in desired accomplishments that can be seen and counted. Prevention outcomes are a decrease in undesired potential occurrences. Developmental outcomes (or DO's, as this is what we should be "DO-ing") are beliefs, behaviors, knowledge and skills that prepare a young person for health and success in adolescence and adulthood. Most youth work approaches focus on achievement or prevention outcomes; that is, they are concerned with what a young person should or shouldn't be doing. The Youth Development approach focuses on developmental outcomes; that is, it is concerned with who and what a young person is becoming. Within the Youth Development field there is not yet agreement on a specific way to define developmental outcomes. The four primary efforts in this regard are the Montessori approach, the Search Institute's 40 Developmental Assets, the 5 (or 6 or 7) C's, and the Advancing Youth Development curriculum. These multiple efforts tend to have more similarities than differences. The *concept* is to focus *more* on who and what a young person is becoming, and *less* on what they are doing or not doing. Achievement and prevention outcomes become a consequence of your practice, rather than its goal.

Lesson 3: (s)OS -- A Framework for Youth Development

 Implementing a Youth Development approach requires a consistent application of the (s)OS framework, which stands for (services) and *Opportunities and Supports.* A (service) is something you do *to* or *for* a young person, and while (services) do not promote development, they may be a necessary foundation for activities that do promote development. *Opportunities and Supports* are things done *by* young people *with* adult support. A Youth Development approach is to reduce (services) to minimum required interventions and replace them with *Opportunities and Supports,* realizing that the goal is not success or failure, but growth and development. Traditional youth work provides success-biased services that result in achievement and prevention outcomes. Positive Youth Development creates Opportunities and provides Supports, allowing for both success and failure to contribute to a young person's growth and development.

Lesson 4: High Expectations

We interact with people offering various conscious and unconscious cues as to our beliefs and expectations. People receiving these cues adjust their behavior to match the cues they are receiving. This is known as the *Pygmalion Effect*. Many of our beliefs and expectations related to young people are negative. To foster resiliency and promote development, we must overcome these negative beliefs and expectations and communicate positive beliefs and messages (High Expectations). This cannot be faked … you actually have to *have* High Expectations of young people; it is something that you need to *believe*.

Lesson 5: Meaningful Participation

Youth participation is a component of the Youth Development approach. To be effective, it must be used as a Protective Factor within the PYD framework. While consumer input benefits the program or service, that is not its goal or purpose. It is the benefit to the young person that is the reason for youth participation, and therefore strategies must be employed that allow all young people to participate appropriate to their level of development. All young people can and will participate if the opportunity is clear, legitimate, and relevant. If young people are not participating the problem is not with the young person, the problem is with the opportunity. Youth participation takes five main forms; Choosing, Decision Making, Assessing or Evaluating, Planning, and Communicating. Care should be taken with Communicating, as some people find it extremely uncomfortable. The four primary strategies for youth participation are Ad Hoc Input, Consultation, Influence, and Partnership.

Lesson 6: Caring, Supportive Relationships

The success of any endeavor is based on mastery of 5 to 9 "core competencies." There is a lack of consensus on the core competencies required for Positive Youth Development. This is probably because PYD is an *approach*, not a *model*. Mastery of 4 basic skills is required to create relationships that will serve as Protective Factors. The 4 basic skills are Attentive Listening (for Ad Hoc Input), Information Sharing (for Consultation), Win/Win Negotiating (for Influence), and Delegation (for Partnership).

All of the answers to the Final Exam crossword puzzle are contained in the review you just completed.

Instructions:

1. Fill in the answers to the 11 clues
2. Unscramble the shared letters to complete the sentence

Across

1. Words that describe a Service
2. (A Protective Factor) Meaningful [fill in]
3. Outcomes that are the focus of PYD
4. (PYD Framework) The last 'S' in (s)OS
5. Word that describes 4 Across
6. Word that describes 4 Down

Down

1. Research base of Youth Development
2. (A Protective Factor) Caring and Supportive [fill in]
3. (A Protective Factor) High:
4. (PYD Framework) The 'O' in (S)OS
5. Achievement and Prevention:

The fisherman hoped to catch many salmon, but caught

___ ___ ___   ___   ___ ___ ___ ___

Special Offer:

If you answered all of the crossword puzzle clues correctly, you ended up with 10 shared letters that when unscrambled complete the fisherman sentence. Send the unscrambled words that complete the sentence <u>in the subject line</u> of an email to jtfest@in4y.com to receive a Certificate of Completion suitable for framing in a printable PDF.

 If you have completed the review and Final Exam crossword puzzle, you may now move on to the Bonus Lessons in the appendices.

APPENDIX A

Bonus Lesson
Measuring Developmental Outcomes

What gets measured gets done.

~ Peter Drucker ~

In this lesson you will learn:

- The impact of what we measure
- Creating indicators and measurements

At the conclusion of **Lesson 2, Youth Outcomes: The "Bottom Line" of Youth Work**, it was stated that an often cited final criticism of PYD is that developmental outcomes are difficult to *measure*. This bonus lesson addresses that criticism and gives you tools for measuring developmental outcomes. It is assumed that you have already completed the 6-lesson Winning Hand Workbook, and are now knowledgeable and skilled enough to begin implementing PYD in your daily practice. By completing this bonus lesson you will be able to prioritize developmental outcomes by having the tools to measure your success.

Before starting this bonus lesson, it will be helpful to consider some additional reflection on how we think about youth outcomes. The following article, written and released prior to the creation of this workbook, expands upon the concepts presented in **Lesson 2 -- Youth Outcomes: The "Bottom Line" of Youth Work**. Please read it before completing this bonus lesson.

An Outlook on Outcomes
The impact of what we measure

*All too often we are giving young people cut flowers
when we should be teaching them to grow their own plants.*

~ John W. Gardner ~

I strongly suspect we can all agree that outcomes are important. When I present the Youth Development approach I describe outcomes as the "bottom line" of youth work. No matter how you work with young people, the value of your work can only be measured in relationship to what *results* from your work.

I also suspect that the fact that outcomes are important may be the *only* area on which we can all agree. Agreeing that outcomes are important doesn't help us to reach consensus on what *types* of outcomes are important, and it certainly doesn't help us determine the most effective ways to measure success in reaching specific outcomes.

This creates a situation where we may *not* agree on what we *do* agree is the most important aspect of our work. To make matters worse, we rarely even get to debate outcomes because, more often than not, outcomes are decided for us.

For the majority of youth services the basis of support is a third-party contract. A private or public source provides the financial support for delivery of the service to the consumer. This sets up an awkward situation right off the bat, as the *consumer* of the service is not the *customer*, and it is the customer who gets to determine outcomes.

When the consumer is not the customer it directly impacts the manner in which outcomes are viewed. For example, let's say I am a customer who is paying a food service to provide daily meals to one thousand people. I'm sure I will be concerned that the meals meet minimal nutritional standards, and I'd also be concerned about the cost of providing the meals. But let's say instead that I'm paying the service to provide meals to *my family and myself*. While I may still be concerned about standards and cost-effectiveness, I'm likely to be *more* concerned about the health and nutrition of the meals beyond minimal standards, the quality of the ingredients, the taste and variety of the menu, and my family's specific culinary likes and dislikes. The simple reality is that outcomes will be different depending on whether the customer is *also* the consumer.

This reality points out a major problem with the current state of many youth outcome requirements. As they have been developed by customers who are *not* consumers, there is a strong influence on cost-effectiveness -- in my opinion to the detriment of other more critical outcomes from the perspective of a young person's needs and development. This problem is compounded by a simple fact: *young people are not cost-effective.*

Need proof? Have a child -- but that might be more than you're willing to invest in this exercise. So instead consider this. According to the United States Department of Agriculture, raising a child from birth through age 17 will cost $241,080.00[19]. That's over $13,393.00 every year, for 18 years. After investing these multiple tens of thousands of dollars, you have bought yourself an 18-year-old ready for college. That means *more* investment. Even a standard 4-year bachelor's degree can cost between about $35,000 and $120,000 *or more* -- and that may be just for tuition. Associated costs can easily run you several grand more a year.

When all is said and done, be prepared to sink somewhere between *three hundred thousand and half a million dollars* into your child. If that financial investment has resulted in an average American child, you now face a 1 in 4 possibility that they will continue to live with you until they are 34.

Now let's consider an example from the youth work field. For this example I'll stick to an area that I'm familiar with; transitional living programs (TLP's) for street-dependent youth. In a TLP we basically have the same responsibility as parents. The young person is living at the program 24/7 and all of their needs are being provided for by the program or through the program's resources. If we use the previously stated numbers, we can expect to spend $13,393.00 per year on each resident and, since a parent's *time* is not included in this figure, this does not include personnel and administrative costs. Therefore, annually a 7-bed facility can expect to spend $93,751.00 in *addition* to the cost of personnel and administration. Since conservatively these costs generally represent 70% and 10% of a TLP's budget respectively, a 7-bed TLP should be funded at about $468,755.00.

There are several things to consider about this figure. The first is that no federal TLP in the nation receives this level of funding. $200,000.00 is the maximum, and many TLP's receive far less. Consider also that, even if a program were receiving the $468,755.00 figure, we are talking about salaries in the $25,000.00 - $35,000.00 range -- salaries which are simply not sufficient to compensate and retain quality employees considering the level of skill required by the program. But that's only the beginning of the story.

Remember that our dollar figures are based on the expenses required by a healthy adolescent who has been raised in a secure, caring family that continues to provide a basis of support. This does not describe the situation of the adolescent we see in programs for at-risk youth. The adolescent we see often has medical and mental health needs that are not considered in the "standard" cost of raising a child. They are often developmentally delayed, lacking adequate support systems and socialization skills, and suffering post-traumatic stress from abuse, neglect, and abandonment.

So, all of this considered, we have a situation where outcomes are dictated by a customer who is not a consumer, predicated on cost-effectiveness with a population that is not cost-effective, and applied to consumers who have greater challenges and obstacles than their peers who end up hanging out at their parent's house until they're 34 and are able to finally figure out what they want to be when they grow up.

As stated at the beginning of this article, though, outcomes *are* important -- regardless of how they are measured they are the "bottom line" of what we do. And, despite my treatise on cost-effectiveness, customers (funding sources) need to determine if they are getting their money's worth. I fully understand this reality, and I have been in social services long enough to know that there can be a tremendous amount of waste. I'm actually a rather big "accountability" kind of guy. My concern is not with measurement *per se*. Rather it is with *what* we chose to measure and the effects of our choices.

Outcome Categories

The three primary categories that all outcomes can be placed in are achievement, prevention, and developmental. Achievement outcomes are tangible accomplishments; e.g., completing school, getting a job, finding stable housing. Prevention outcomes are avoidance of problem behaviors; e.g., pregnancy, drug abuse, violence. Developmental outcomes are beliefs, behaviors, knowledge, and skills; e.g., self-worth, responsibility and autonomy, employability.

It should be clear from these definitions why the overwhelming majority of outcomes required by funding sources fall into the achievement and prevention categories. If you are counting the pennies you invest and looking at what they're buying, it is natural to focus on accomplishments and preventing problems; to focus on things we *want* young people to do or the things we *don't* want them to do (or both). These aren't bad things. Young people completing school, getting jobs, avoiding early pregnancy, and staying away from violence and drugs -- who can argue with these outcomes? Certainly not me, and my caution is not about the outcomes themselves … it is about *focusing* on them.

There is a law that rears its ugly head from time to time with which I'm sure many of you have had personal experience. It is not a human law, it is a *natural* law, making it all that more difficult to avoid. I'm referring to the Law of Unintended Consequences, and the truly devious aspect of this law is that it tends to hide behind good intentions. This is why debate is so critical in our field, because everything we do is based in good intentions, but good intentions are not enough -- we also have to have good results. As mentioned earlier in this article we rarely *debate* outcomes. We more often than not simply try to achieve what our customers are purchasing, and in so doing we unleash the Law of Unintended Consequences on our young consumers.

Focusing on achievement and prevention outcomes completely misses the point of what young people need. Do the young people you work with need jobs, or education, or housing? Do they need to avoid pregnancy, or violence, or drugs? Before you answer "yes" consider the following.

Imagine that a young person has developed beliefs and behaviors that demonstrate personal well-being and a sense of connection and commitment to others. They think of themselves as a "good" person with something of value to contribute, and they feel that they are succeeding in life. They feel safe in the world and can create a personal structure that makes daily events somewhat predictable. They are able to exercise some control over their lives and are accountable for their actions. They are able to differentiate themselves while maintaining attachment to community and higher beliefs and principles.

Now also imagine that they possess knowledge and skills that give them the ability and motivation to ensure current and future success. They have the ability to gain the necessary skills for employment, and they are able to learn, think, problem-solve, and study independently. They respect differences among groups and individuals and are able to work collaboratively and sustain relationships. Additionally, they are motivated to ensure current and future physical health and know how to cope with situations and engage in leisure and fun.

Would you need to find this imagined youth a job? Would you need to get them off of drugs, or deal with their issues of violence? Would you need to encourage them to finish school? Probably not, because the young person I described is unlikely to be engaging in risk behaviors, and is motivated to complete school and find employment on their own.

The above description represents the outcomes we look for in young people when we focus on their development. When focusing on developmental outcomes we don't need to focus on achievement and prevention because such things are a natural *consequence* of a young person's healthy development. In fact, it's not that achievement and prevention is unimportant, it's that it is *too* important to make it the focus of our work because, when we do, we open the door for the Law of Unintended Consequences.

Unintended Consequences of Achievement and Prevention

No outcomes are easier to obtain than achievement and prevention. This is a problem, because the easier they become, the greater the disservice we do to the young people with whom we work. Let me correct myself just slightly. It's not that achievement and prevention outcomes are easy, it's that there are *shortcuts*; easy ways to their realization. For example; do you want to get a young person off of drugs? Easy. Lock him or her up for 30 days. Goal accomplished, they're off drugs. Of course, whether or not they stay off drugs after release is a huge question, but the program may have successfully accomplished its fundable goal. How about securing employment for a young person? Easy. Locate a job and place your young person in the position. Goal accomplished, they're employed. Of course, within a week they may tell the boss to stick it where the sun don't shine and rejoin the ranks of the unemployed, but, again, the program may have accomplished its fundable goal.

These two examples highlight the potential problem with tying funding to achievement and prevention outcomes. It provides incentive for programs to take shortcuts in order to obtain the measurable outcome that justifies continued support. This is particularly true when we are trying to crank out short-term outcomes, such as taking a young person who is coming from an 18 year history of abuse, neglect, poverty, and educational failure and attempting to make them independent and self-supporting in weeks or months, years before their stable, healthy peers are able to accomplish the same outcome. The result is that we are more focused on meeting *our* needs to justify the dollars than we are on meeting the young person's *developmental* needs, and guess who loses in that scenario?

Why do we so often see young people as failures and incompetent? Why do we see high recidivism rates, and why does follow-up reveal such a high rate of inability to *maintain* successful outcomes? Could it be because we are pushing outcomes that are ahead of a young person's *development*? And could that be because we are pursuing the wrong types of outcomes to begin with?

Unfortunately, increased outcome dissatisfaction may give birth to responses that exasperate the problem. Such is the case with performance-based contracting. If you are not familiar, performance-based contracting is the idea that a program will receive a certain percentage of funding for providing services (it varies, but usually in the 60% to 70% range), and the remainder of the funding will only be paid based on outcome measurement -- the same achievement and prevention measurements the program was struggling to obtain under the old system of contracting. While the good intention here is to guarantee that services are working for young people, the whole concept is based on the faulty premise (in my opinion) that failure to obtain achievement and prevention outcomes in the short-term is a result of incompetent services. All performance-based contracting does is "up the ante" in terms of creating incentives for shortcuts, as well as increasing another unintended consequence of the achievement and prevention focus; *creaming*.

Creaming is the tendency of programs to gradually evolve to serving higher functioning youth. If a program must demonstrate short-term accomplishments in order to survive, it will naturally begin to serve only those young people who are developmentally able to succeed in the short-term. The more "difficult" youth eventually gets screened out of services because he or she needs too much or takes too long. The ultimate end result is that we are spending all of our dollars on youth who don't really need the help, and none of our dollars on those who do -- at least, none of our service dollars; we certainly still pay the tab in social and legal costs.

The irony is that, for all of our focus on cost-effectiveness, we end up with the most cost-*ineffective* system one could imagine, and we repeat this mistake in cycles. I have been around long enough to see grassroots services start up to meet the needs of the "difficult" and underserved youth, only to evolve to serving the higher functioning youth in order to demonstrate fundable outcomes. New grassroots agencies then appear to serve the more "difficult" youth the previous agencies *used* to serve. Throughout this process, young people who really need assistance are the ones least likely to get it.

A New Outcome Focus

I suggest that any attempts at outcome measurement and program accountability are doomed to failure until we change our outcome focus. To this end, I recommend two major shifts in outcome measurement and accountability.

1. Focus on development, not achievement or prevention

   I am a strong advocate of the Youth Development approach, mainly because it is research based, and it works. One of the primary tenets of this approach is that perceived problems are not the issue. Rather, "problems" are symptoms of unmet developmental needs. If this is true (and I propose that it is), then a problem-focus is just a *symptom-*focus … what we need to do is to cure the disease. Outcome measurements, therefore, should not focus on the traditional jobs, education, and/or delinquent behaviors. They should instead focus on young people's development.

2. Measure the provider, not the young people

   Remember the customer/consumer separation discussed earlier? One difficulty affecting outcomes is that, in effect, we have the customer holding the employee (programs) accountable to the *consumer's* behavior. What makes better sense is for the customer to hold the employee accountable to its *own* behavior.

Resiliency research has shown that young people's development flourishes in an environment of Protective Factors, and we know that assisting a young person in their developmental process is the path to meaningful and lasting achievement and prevention outcomes. That being said, the customer should hold the employee accountable to *the manner in which they are providing services.* Instead of measuring a program's success by what *young people* are doing or not doing, success would be measured by what a *program* is doing or not doing, grounded in the research-based knowledge of how Protective Factor environments foster a young person's innate resiliency, enabling them to accomplish achievement and prevention outcomes according to their capacity and developmental readiness rather than an artificial timeline based on meeting pre-determined outcome measurements.

Interestingly, using this approach, achievement and prevention outcomes could still be measured over time as an indicator of a program's long term effectiveness, but the tie to funding would be on the program's *activities* rather than the young person's *outcomes.* This change in focus would free programs from the pressures that lead to creaming, shortcuts, and outright manipulation of outcome data, and allow them to focus instead on the specific developmental needs of the young people seeking their services.

Conclusion

Management consultant Peter Drucker once stated "What gets measured gets done." If we measure our success by a youth's performance, we can expect programs to focus on performance above all else, resulting in the unintended consequences described above and ultimately failing the young people we serve. If we measure our performance based on researched and proven practice that we know meets the developmental needs of young people, then, ironically, we can expect to see greater success in reaching the achievement and prevention goals that we currently measure. Is such a change in focus likely to happen? Sadly, perhaps not, but that doesn't mean that it's not worth advocating. [end of article]

Indicators and Measurements

Everything discussed concerning developmental outcomes in Winning Hand is pointless if there is no way for us to determine if we are being successful in our attempts to assist young people in their developmental process. In this regard, developmental outcomes are no different than achievement or prevention outcomes. No matter what type of outcomes you desire, you need some way to know whether or not you're getting what you're seeking.

With achievement and prevention outcomes, a fairly straightforward method can be used to track your progress. It is simply a matter of creating a system of *indicators* and *measurements*. An *indicator* is something you identify as a sign that you are getting your desired results. Simply, it is the answer to the question: How do you know? A *measurement* is something you identify for evaluation or as basis for comparison. It is a method of quantifying your results. Simply, it is the answer to the question: How do you document? For example, if you have an educational program that measures its success by students graduating (an achievement outcome), your *indicator* of success is a student's graduation, and your *measurement* of success is how many students graduate. If 8 out of 10 students graduate, your program is 80% successful. How can you measure developmental outcomes, however, where you are focused on who and what a young person is becoming, rather than what they are or are not doing? The answer is as easy and as difficult as; you measure them the exact same way that you measure achievement and prevention outcomes, by creating a system of *indicators* and *measurements*.

The easy part is that we don't have to learn a new method of measuring outcomes. The difficult part is that we are not used to looking at development through the lens of indicators and measurements. But to successfully implement a Youth Development approach, you must first create a system of indicators and measurements related to developmental outcomes.

There are three legitimate questions that you may have at this point:

1. Why is it important to create indicators and measurements for developmental outcomes? Can't I just focus on developmental outcomes, and measure the resulting expected increase in achievement and prevention outcomes?

    This is an excellent question. The greater your success in focusing on development, the greater the odds are that you will see achievement and prevention outcomes as a consequence. However, this will only happen if your practice maintains a focus on developmental outcomes; and without related indicators and measurements, your practice will lose that focus.

    Our practice is driven by our intention, and our intention is a reflection of what we are looking at and thinking about. We will naturally look at and think about what we *measure*. The well-known writer, management consultant, and university professor Peter Drucker said "What gets measured gets done." I would paraphrase this statement as *what gets measured, gets focused on*, and what we focus on drives what we practice.

    A brief story might help illustrate the point. A friend of mine took a course to learn how to ride a motorcycle. Her instructor told her that there would come a time when she was taking a corner and she would feel like she was going too fast and losing control of the bike. When this happens, she should *focus her eyes on where she wants the bike to go*. A few weeks later, she found herself in that very situation. She remembered what her instructor told her, but off to her left was a nasty looking ditch that had her concerned. She really didn't want to end up in the ditch and, as a result, she kept her eyes on the ditch. I'm sure you can guess what happened next.

    My friend ended up in the ditch because that's what she was focused on. By the same principle, if all we measure is achievement and prevention, we will fall off the road of Youth Development and end up back in the "ditch" we were in before we began implementation.

In order to successfully implement PYD we need to keep our focus on developmental outcomes, and to do that we need to have associated indicators and measurements.

2. Why do I have to create my own indicators and measurements?

It would be nice if I could just give you a list of indicators and measurements for you to follow, but there are two reasons why you need to develop your own, and one reason why it's preferable.

To begin with the first two reasons, remember that at this point in the PYD field there isn't even agreement on how to present developmental outcomes, let alone measure them. The first thing you need to do is to decide what presentation of developmental outcomes works for you. Winning Hand prefers the modified presentation originally created for the Advancing Youth Development curriculum in Lesson 2, and this is the presentation used throughout this workbook. But you may find that the 5 (or 6 or 7) C's, or the Search Institute's 40 Developmental Assets, or the Montessori Method, or something *you* create, better meets your needs.

After you have decided what you're going to measure, you'll need to determine what the indicators and measurements would look like within your *model*. Remember, Youth Development is an *approach*, not a *model*. If I were to give you indicators for measuring an increase in the developmental outcome related to Mastery and Future that were developed for a street outreach program, they may not be at all similar to how the indicators might appear within a job training program. Even if you are using the same presentation of developmental outcomes, the indicators and measurements may not be transferable from one program *model* to another.

That being said, from a practice perspective, it is also preferable that you develop your own indicators and measurements. Focusing on developmental outcomes is difficult within a funding and service system that sees primarily achievement and prevention. The ability to do so is the most significant cognitive shift that practitioners must make when implementing PYD, and the inability to make the shift is the single biggest reason why PYD efforts may be unsuccessful. The exercise of creating indicators and measurements for developmental outcomes serves to reinforce the concepts, focus the attention, and support implementation efforts.

3. How do I go about creating indicators and measurements for developmental outcomes?

As previously stated, the first step is to decide how you're going to present developmental outcomes. Regardless of the presentation you choose, the process after that is the same. For this workbook we are using the presentation created for the Advancing Youth Development curriculum, but this process is applicable to any presentation of developmental outcomes.

STOP **Before you proceed** ... Imagine that you work with at-risk youth and have been asked to justify your funding to a group of people who know very little about the youth with whom you work. You are trying to get them to understand the *environments* (e.g., poverty, unstable housing) that these young people have grown up in, and the *experiences* (e.g., abuse, school failure) they've had growing up. You are not talking about character traits, or skills, or potential, or actions on their part, rather you are describing *environments* and *experiences*. Follow the instructions below.

Instructions: For **2 minutes** (use a timer) list below as many environments or experiences that you can think of that may be applicable to your youth. It is OK to generalize, not every youth you've known will have been in every environment or had every experience -- but you want to make sure that people have a good general understanding of the types of environments and experiences that your youth as a population have had in their backgrounds. Begin this exercise now.

Environments	Experiences

GO Look at the lists you created. While there may be some differences, it is likely a list of pretty scary things, particularly for a young person. Most lists I've seen include various forms of abuse including physical, sexual, and emotional. Domestic and neighborhood (gang) violence often appear, as well as poverty and unstable housing. You may have included drug abuse and alcoholism, or other criminal activities to which the young person was exposed. Undoubtedly your list includes items such as these and many other very frightening things for a child to experience.

Now, imagine that you are a child from these environments and with these experiences as your reference points. The list you created is your *knowledge of life on Earth*. What do you think might be one of your dominant feelings? You may say anger, or hyper-vigilance, or a number of other emotions, but the truth is that the primary emotion you would be walking around with all of the time is *fear*. The world is an unpredictable, dangerous, and *frightening* place.

 Before you proceed … Forget about young people for the moment and just focus on your knowledge of human behavior. Follow the instructions below.

Instructions: For **2 minutes** (use a timer) describe below all of the different types of behaviors you might expect to see in a human being who is currently acting from a place of fear. If there was a person in front of you right now who was fearful, what are some of the ways that you might anticipate they'd behave?

_____ _____

_____ _____

_____ _____

_____ _____

_____ _____

_____ _____

GO Look at the list you created. While there may be some differences, it is likely a long list of behaviors running the gamut from aggressiveness, anger and distrust, to withdrawn, submissive or even suicidal. The reason for this long and diverse list of behaviors is because we as human beings are hard-wired in how we react to fear.

In Lesson 1 we first talked about the fact that we humans are "hard-wired" in certain ways, such as with our will to survive or to be resilient in the face of adversity. When it comes to fear, we are hard-wired to react with *fight* or *flight* (Note: please review Footnote 10). In other words, as soon as we feel fearful, we respond to that feeling of fear with a two-step process:

Step One: Identify a source for the fear

It's important to understand that the source a person identifies may not be the actual source of their fear. Sometimes people feel fear for no conscious reason -- they may be reacting to past events or traumas. However, our minds do not allow us to feel fear and not identify a source because we are about to go into fight or flight, and we have to know what to fight or flee from. So it may be the actual source of our fear, such as a truck about to run us over; or a projected source of our fear, such as a smiling youth worker saying "good morning." In either case, we will then decide whether to fight it or flee from it.

Step Two: Fight or Flight

The decision between fight or flight is based upon our assessment of the most effective means we see to *eliminate the source of the fear* as quickly as possible. In some cases, like a truck bearing down on you, fight is simply not an option, so we will choose flight and try to get out of the way. In other situations, the decision could go either way and may be made moment to moment. In other words, we may start with fight behavior and see that we can't destroy the source, so we move to flight behavior until we see that we can't get away from the source, so we return to fight behavior. While we may switch back and forth, each of these behaviors has a specific means to the same end. With the decision to fight our means is to destroy (or at least neutralize) the source as quickly as possible. When we choose flight our means is to get away from the source as quickly as possible. With either decision, the end is the same -- no longer be threatened by the source in order to alleviate the feeling of fear.

Each of the behaviors you listed can be categorized into either fight or flight behavior based on whether it is attacking the source or avoiding the source. Behaviors such as aggressiveness, anger and distrust are generally fight behaviors, while behaviors such as withdrawal, submissiveness and suicide are generally flight behaviors.

 Before you proceed ... Look at the list of fear-based behaviors that you created. Think about each one and try to categorize it as a fight or flight behavior.

You probably had a relatively easy time categorizing the behaviors by fight or flight. Some may have been challenging, and others may have arguably gone into either category, but generally speaking the behaviors were fairly easy to group. Why? Because these behaviors are motivated by a specific need -- the need to feel safe. Therefore these behaviors are *indicators* of a person who does not feel safe.

I should point out that you may have noticed something else about your list, particularly if you work with trauma-impacted youth on a regular basis. You may have noticed that the behaviors on your list look very *familiar*. You probably see these types of behaviors in the young people with whom you work. And it is here where Youth Development has a very different focus from traditional youth service approaches, because traditionally these behaviors are seen as *the problem*. The *problem* is that the young person is too aggressive or too withdrawn, and interventions are employed to "fix" the *problem*. The Youth Development perspective, however, is that these behaviors are not *problems*; they are *indicators* of a developmental need. Look again at the Advancing Youth Development curriculum's presentation of developmental outcomes (see the Youth Outcomes Chart in Appendix B). One of the outcomes listed under Aspects of Identity is **Safety and Structure**, or the need to feel safe in the world and know that daily events are somewhat predictable. When you see a young person demonstrating fight or flight behaviors, you are not looking at a young person with *problems*; you are looking at a young person with an unmet developmental need to feel safe in the world.

These observable, documentable behaviors become indicators of progress toward the developmental need for safety. If you see these behaviors escalating, the young person is feeling less safe by your efforts and you should try something else. If these behaviors are moderating, then do more of whatever you're doing. Your indicators of success with Safety and Structure are the observable fight or flight behaviors, and your measurement of success is documentation of these behaviors moderating.

This is the process to use for all developmental outcomes. If a young person were to show improvement in a specific area of focus, how would you know? How would they behave differently? And once you know what you are looking for, how will it be documented?

Another example comes from my experience with streetwork. For many years I did street-based case management with street-dependent youth. This meant an office without walls where I would arrange to meet them in a park or a fast food restaurant. I figured out early on that an absolutely indispensable item in my outreach kit was a good book -- because I was spending a lot of time in these places by myself waiting for a youth to show up as it was very common for them to forget about or just blow off the appointment. One of the first developmental outcomes I needed to work on was **Responsibility and Autonomy**, or the need for them to exercise control over daily events and be accountable for their actions and the consequences of their actions. If I couldn't help them with that, I'd be spending a lot of time by myself.

So how did I know if I was helping? One of the methods was to simply define keeping appointments and being on time as an *indicator*. I could then measure these indicators and track change over time. Maybe during the first few months that I was seeing a youth they would blow me off 70% of the time and were late 80% of the time that they did show up. But maybe after 6 months I noticed that they'd blowing me off only 40% of the time and late only 20% of the time. And maybe after 8 months I'm seeing them make and keep appointments with me as well as other services. In other words, I could document progress toward a developmental outcome by identifying and tracking behaviors associated with that outcome. If after x-number of months I was seeing no or negative change, I'd know that what I was doing wasn't working, and I'd best try something else. That, by the way, is one of the Prime Directives of youth work; if what you're doing isn't working, *stop doing that and do something else.*

The examples above show not only the process of looking at developmental outcomes through an indicator and measurement lens, but they also point out a critical cognitive shift. A young person who is demonstrating aggressiveness and violence is not seen as a bad kid who needs his behavior "fixed." Instead he is seen as a young person who doesn't feel safe, and his behaviors are normal, rational, and predictable indicators of his need for safety. A young person who misses or is late for appointments is not seen as irresponsible or unmotivated, or unwilling to take steps to improve her life. Instead she is seen as a young woman who needs help learning how to exercise control over daily events and see the connection between cause and effect. It is a shift from seeing the behaviors as evidence of "problems" that need to be fixed, to seeing them as *normal* behaviors that indicate where a young person can use your help with their development.

Measuring in the Short Term

A legitimate criticism is that measuring developmental outcomes is a long term process. Sometimes you don't have the luxury of working with individual youth over a period of months or years and, even if you do, it is extremely helpful to have short term measurements to ensure that you are moving toward the long term outcomes you are seeking. The good news is that there is a way to create such assurance on a daily basis, but it involves looking *inward* rather than outward.

In Lesson 1 we learned that to foster a young person's healthy development we need to foster their innate capacity for resiliency, and the way we foster their innate capacity for resiliency is to create Protective Factor environments around them. Therefore, if you want to measure your short term progress toward long term goals, the most effective way to do it is to measure *your* success at creating Protective Factors in a young person's life.

Many organizations have adopted a Youth Development construct called The Five Promises. These "Promises" indicate developmental resources/supports that young people need for success in their lives. The Five Promises are Caring Adults, Safe Places, A Healthy Start, Effective Education, and Opportunities to Serve. Clearly two of these Five Promises directly correspond to two of the three Protective Factors; Caring, Supportive Relationships (Caring Adults) and Meaningful Participation (Opportunities to Serve). The third Protective Factor -- High Expectations -- is perhaps assumed within the three promises of Safe Places, A Healthy Start, and Effective Education, though these three promises focus more on addressing specific developmental needs[20] than they do Protective Factors. Still, The Five Promises serve as a good framework for a daily activity focus and, when considered with the three Protective Factors, can provide short term measures of your success at implementing behaviors that are directly linked to longer term developmental outcomes.

Keeping your daily activity focus on Protective Factors and The Five Promises is the best way to ensure progress toward developmental outcomes. The "Contact Record" on the next page is a tool by which you can reflect upon your practice. After any significant contact with a young person, take a few minutes to (honestly) reflect upon your behavior (not the young person's), and record your thoughts as applicable.

Protective Factors/Five Promises Contact Record

Youth Identifier: _____ Date: _____

Enhanced our relationship:
How did I strengthen, enhance, clarify or deepen your relationship?

What did I do today?	*What can I do in the future?*

Fostered connections/relationships with others:
How did I establish, strengthen, enhance, clarify or deepen the youth's relationship with others.

What did I do today?	*What can I do in the future?*

Demonstrated High/Low Expectations:
List actions taken and the message those actions communicated. List actions that communicated both high and low expectations for the greatest learning. List messages to communicate in the future as well as actions that will communicate that message.

What did I do?	*What was the message?*
What message would I like to send?	*What would communicate that message?*

Addressed Safety:
"Addressed" can range from awareness to action. "Safety" can be psycho-emotional or physical.

What did I do today?	*What can I do in the future?*

Addressed Health:
"Addressed" can range from awareness to action. "Health" can be psycho-emotional or physical.

What did I do today?	*What can I do in the future?*

Inspired Learning:
"Inspired" includes formal and traditional education-related activities, but may also include anything that encourages greater knowledge.

What did I do today?	*What can I do in the future?*

Created Opportunity for Meaningful Participation:
For each opportunity, identify how it was clear, legitimate, and relevant.

How did s/he participate?	*How did I ensure clarity?*	*How was it legitimate?*	*How was it relevant?*

Summation

- Developmental outcomes are measurable, and, while they should result in greater achievement and prevention outcomes, it is important to measure them independently as a way of keeping your practice consistent with the Youth Development approach.
- Developmental outcomes can be tracked using the same approach of indicators and measurements that are used to track achievement and prevention outcomes.
- *Indicators* are observable signs that you are getting your desired results. Simply, they are the answer to the question: How do you know?
- *Measurements* are a method of quantifying your results. Simply, they are the answer to the question: How do you document?
- Indicators and measurements need to be created for each developmental outcome you wish to impact, ensuring that those indicators and measurements are applicable and relevant to the model in which you interact with young people.
- Short term measurements should be focused on your fidelity to the creation of Protective Factor environments and The Five Promises.

 Bonus Lesson Learning Assignment

Part 1: For this exercise you will be using the Indicators and Measurements Worksheets that follow. Working by yourself, or with your colleagues, or with one or more young people (19 or younger), or any combination of these groups, follow the instructions on the worksheets and complete the assignment. Please note the following:

- It is likely that this assignment will take you more than one session. To get the most out of this exercise, be prepared to engage in multiple sessions over time. Due to the on-going nature of this assignment, it is not necessary to complete Part 1 before completing Part 2
- It is also likely that the assignment may turn into a "work in progress" and become more of an on-going project rather than a task that is "completed." Permission is granted to make copies of these worksheets in preparation for multiple updates and revisions.

Part 2: Meet with your supervisor (or adult learning partner) and discuss the following questions. Write the key points of your discussion below:

1. What did you learn from the Bonus Lesson and/or the worksheet exercise that was new for you?

_____

_____

_____

2. What did you re-learn or remember as a result of the Bonus Lesson and/or the worksheet exercise?

_____

_____

_____

3. List the key thoughts, points, or ideas that you want to remember from the Bonus Lesson and/or the worksheet exercise. You may list as many items as you wish, but list at least <u>3</u>.

_____

_____

_____

GO Use the following worksheets to complete Part 1 of this Bonus Lesson:

The Winning Hand Workbook

Indicators and Measurements
WORKSHEET I
ASPECTS OF IDENTITY

Instructions: For each developmental outcome below, create a list of indicators and measurements that are applicable and relevant to your setting. Feel free to use additional paper or to create a different form using a different list of developmental outcomes if you wish (the 5 C's, for example).

OUTCOME A sense of personal well-being and connection/commitment to others	INDICATORS How will you know?	MEASUREMENTS How will you document?
Self-Worth: ▪ One is a "good person" ▪ Contributes to self and others		
Safety and Structure: ▪ One is safe in the world ▪ Daily events are somewhat predictable		
Belonging and Membership: ▪ Values, and is valued by, others in the family and community		
Responsibility and Autonomy: ▪ Some control over daily events ▪ Accountable for actions and consequences		
Mastery and Future: ▪ One is "making it" ▪ Will succeed in the future		
Self-Awareness and Spirituality: ▪ One is unique, intimately attached to extended families, cultural groups, communities, higher deities, principles		

Modified by JT Fest from original source: AED/Center for Youth Development and Policy Research

The Winning Hand Workbook

Indicators and Measurements
WORKSHEET II
AREAS OF ABILITY

Instructions: For each developmental outcome below, create a list of indicators and measurements that are applicable and relevant to your setting. Feel free to use additional paper or to create a different form using a different list of developmental outcomes if you wish (the 5 C's, for example).

OUTCOME Knowledge, skills and attitudes that prepare youth for adulthood	INDICATORS How will you know?	MEASUREMENTS How will you document?
Mental Health: ▪ Ability/motivation to respond to and cope with situations and emotions		
Physical Health: ▪ Ability/motivation to ensure current and future physical health		
Intellectual Ability: ▪ Ability/motivation to think critically, learn, and problem-solve		
Employability: ▪ Ability/motivation to gain skills necessary for employment		
Civic and Social Ability: ▪ Ability/motivation to work collaboratively and sustain relationships		
Cultural Ability: ▪ Ability/motivation to respect and respond to diversity		

Modified by JT Fest from original source: AED/Center for Youth Development and Policy Research

APPENDIX B

Youth Outcomes Chart

Youth Development seeks outcomes related to a young person's development	**"DO's"** Developmental Outcomes	beliefs, behaviors, knowledge, and skills that result in a healthy and accomplished adolescence and adulthood

⇩

Aspects of Identity ⇨	Beliefs and Behaviors - personal well-being - connection to others	Knowledge and Skills - for current and future success	**Areas of** ⇦ **Ability** *ability and motivation …*
Self-worth ⇨ ☐	I am "good" and I contribute to others and myself	… to cope with situations and to engage in leisure and fun	**Mental Health** ⇦ ☐
Safety and Structure ⇨ ☐	I am safe in the world and daily events are somewhat predictable	… to ensure current and future physical health	**Physical Health** ⇦ ☐
Belonging and Membership ⇨ ☐	I value and am valued by others in my family and in my community	… to learn, think, create, problem-solve, and study independently	**Intellectual Ability** ⇦ ☐
Responsibility and Autonomy ⇨ ☐	I have some control over daily events and am accountable for my actions and their consequences	… to gain the knowledge and skills necessary for employment	**Employability** ⇦ ☐
Mastery and Future ⇨ ☐	I am "making it" and will succeed	… to work collaboratively and to sustain relationships	**Civic and Social Ability** ⇦ ☐
Self-awareness and Spirituality ⇨ ☐	I am unique while attached to families, communities, and higher beliefs and principles	… to appreciate and respect differences among groups and individuals	**Cultural Ability** ⇦ ☐

Traditional Outcome Measures

	Achievement Outcomes ⇧ Increased tangible results ⇧	**Prevention Outcomes** ⇩ Decreased future problems ⇩	
☐			☐

Modified by author from original source: AED Center for Youth Development and Policy Research

APPENDIX C:

Red Flags -- A self-assessment for youth workers

Self-development is a higher duty than self-sacrifice.

~ Elizabeth Cady Stanton ~

Arguably one of the most critical factors affecting your success with a Youth Development approach are the beliefs, values, and attitudes you hold concerning young people. Lesson 4 described the impact of High Expectations and the Pygmalion Effect, yet we live in an adult-dominated culture in which negative stereotypes of youth are so pervasive that we often aren't even aware of them. Regardless of what you may think you believe about young people, you can't help but lean towards the negative unless you actively and consciously make yourself aware of the effect an adult culture has on you. This is particularly true when you are working with at-risk and other marginalized youth populations, whose attitudes and behaviors may seem to confirm many of our culture's negative beliefs about young people.

The following 5 questions are designed to help you examine your own beliefs and attitudes, and keep yourself in check regarding the messages you are sending. Periodically asking these questions of yourself will help you to examine your behavior in relation to what you believe, or think you believe, about young people.

RED FLAG #1: Do you think that you have overcome your negative beliefs about young people and have no further need to examine your attitudes and values in this area?

> **Comments**: Many of you reading this may be committed advocates for youth, with nothing but respect and admiration in your hearts. But at this point in history, achieving complete freedom from negative beliefs about young people is simply not realistic, no matter how much of an advocate you may be. Adults control the dominant culture and that culture is permeated with negative beliefs and stereotypes about our youth. Regardless of what you believe consciously, the dominant culture creates *sub-conscious beliefs and values* that you can't escape.

> Consider this example; when an adult is treated with disrespect, condescended to, patronized, or not given a chance to show what they can do before someone relieves them of responsibility, it is common to

hear the statement "stop treating me like a child." When hearing that statement most of us don't react -- it is simply accepted. But, just for a moment, change the statement. Say instead "stop treating me like a woman" or "stop treating me like an African-American." I hope that you would never dream of making a statement like that, and that people would call you on it if you did. To make that statement would reveal your prejudice against a group of people, show how little faith you have in their capabilities, and how low you hold them in your esteem. So why do we feel comfortable making that statement about children?

Overcoming our prejudices against young people is an on-going struggle, and most of the culture that you live in will support your prejudice, not your struggle. If you ever get to the point where you think that you've got your attitude licked -- **RED FLAG** -- because it's simply not realistic.

RED FLAG #2: To what degree do you experience young people in terms of their problems, deficits, or failure to live up to your expectations?

Comments: Check in with yourself at the end of the day. What was your experience of the young people with whom you worked? Are you aware of their problems, difficulties, and deficits? Are you frustrated and concerned because they are falling short of what you would like to see them achieve? Do you feel drained and overwhelmed from the challenges you faced with them?

Or did you enjoy the time that you spent with them? Are you in awe of their energy, creativity, and humor? Do you feel refreshed and vitalized from the experiences you shared?

In every interaction you have with young people (or any age person, for that matter) there will be peaks and valleys, positives and negatives, joys and sorrows. The question to ask yourself is; which side did you experience? If you find that you experience the deficits to a greater degree than the assets -- **RED FLAG**. The assets are there, too -- if you're looking for them.

RED FLAG #3: When you speak about young people, do you use more negative descriptors than positive ones?

Comments: Listen to yourself as you speak about the young people with whom you work. Are you using terms like manipulative, resistant, and aggressive? Or are you instead using terms such as resourceful, independent, and assertive? Note that these very different terms can be describing the same observable behaviors. Young people trying to meet their needs by working available systems may be described as manipulative or resourceful. They don't like the case plan you've designed? That could mean that they're resistant or independent. They get in your face if they don't like the way they're being treated? Does that make them aggressive or assertive?

Pay attention to the way you identify behaviors. If you find that you are more likely to use a negative descriptor than the corresponding positive one -- **RED FLAG** -- because almost any behavior can be interpreted as a negative or a positive, depending on what beliefs and values you hold related to young people.

RED FLAG #4: Are you unaware of other's use of negative descriptors when they speak of young people?

Comments: Listen to others as they speak about young people. This is the other side of **RED FLAG #3**, because others have the choice between negative interpretations of behavior and positive ones, just as you do. The question to ask yourself in this case, however, is; when you hear negative descriptors of young people, do you really hear them? Are you aware that they may be unfairly judging the behavior of the young people being discussed, or are you unaware that you may be listening to a jaded perception?

I've had the experience of walking out of meetings frustrated by the way young people were discussed. Yet when I speak about it with co-workers who attended the same meeting they don't seem to have noticed that virtually every descriptor used was a negative one.

This is a tough one because you have to notice that you're not noticing. But if you are able to notice that you are not noticing -- **RED FLAG** -- it may be time to increase your awareness.

RED FLAG #5: Do you leave negative statements or stereotypes about young people unchallenged, or find yourself participating in humor and negative stereotyping at the expense of young people?

Comments: Even if you are aware of it when other people make negative statements or stereotype young people, if you don't challenge what you hear, you are, by default, perpetuating the problem. Consider whether or not you would be comfortable sitting in a meeting where your colleagues are being racist, sexist, or homophobic -- even in a mild form or light-hearted manner. If you would not be comfortable in that situation, if you would feel a need to speak up and let them know that their attitude is not acceptable to you -- then why would you accept less of yourself as an advocate for youth?

And you certainly would not participate. So why would you join in joking or stereotyping at a young person's expense? Granted, there are appropriate times when humor can be a release, but far too often we allow ourselves to participate in conversations such as these at times that may not be appropriate. This is an issue for supervisors to note. If you observe one of your staff joining with the crowd when young people are being disparaged it may be something that you want to discuss with them.

When you are around people who are voicing negative beliefs about young people you should be uncomfortable, you should challenge their beliefs, and you should -- above all -- not participate yourself. If you notice that this is not what you do -- **RED FLAG** -- because if you are not an active agent of change, you are simply another part of the problem.

APPENDIX D

Spectrum of Youth Participation -- An Evolutionary View

Strategy ⇨	Ad Hoc Input	Consultation	Influence	Partnership
Time Commitment[21]	← Less Time Commitment		Greater Time Commitment →	
Developmental Outcomes	← Less Impact		Greater Impact →	
Involvement of Youth	← Less Involvement		Greater Involvement →	
Numbers of Youth	Greater Numbers →		← Smaller Numbers	
Concept:	Seek, hear, respect, value, and consider the views and concerns of young people	Structures seeking youth opinions on specific needs, targeted issues, or known situations	Formal processes ensuring a direct link to authority, and at least a minimal impact on decisions	Opportunities with defined responsibilities for specific activities, tasks, or functions
Implications:	An environment seeing and including youth as *contributors to*, not just *recipients of*	A sharing of ideas and information within an environment that is less *us/them* and more *we*	Young people have *real* bargaining power that cannot be negated or circumvented	Young people are responsible and accountability for all or many of the important aspects of a defined area
Ideas:	▪ Individual talks ▪ Workshops or events ▪ Formal policies and procedures for grievance and feedback ▪ Meetings to share and interpret input	▪ General or issue-specific forums, workshops and discussion groups ▪ Focus or reference groups	▪ Advisory groups or councils with a formal charge ▪ Integration of young people into existing structures ▪ Agreements and processes ensuring youth influence	▪ Identified roles or jobs ▪ Youth training, evaluation, and oversight ▪ Youth-lead projects, with adult advice or guidance
Advantages:	▪ Involvement of large number of youth ▪ Participation from children or marginalized young people	▪ Enables direct input by youth ▪ Exploration of issues in depth is enhanced	▪ Young people directly linked with decisions ▪ Significant developmental benefits for the youth involved	▪ Youth have real responsibility ▪ Youth develop ownership of the processes and solutions
Disadvantages:	▪ Input is indirect and interpreted by adults ▪ Sense of ownership is extremely limited	▪ No guarantee of real impact ▪ May create expectations for results and frustration if expectations are not met	▪ Meeting structures may need adaptation ▪ May require young people to fit into adult structures	▪ Confusion over authority can cause conflicts ▪ Involves taking risks/trusting young people to succeed, fail, learn and grow

A Spectrum of Youth Participation: An Evolutionary View was prepared by JT Fest based on Strategies for Youth Participation by Gill Westhorp of the Youth Sector Training Council, Australia; the Australian Youth Foundation; Advancing Youth Development by the AED/Center for Youth Development and Policy Research in collaboration with the National Network for Youth, Inc.; and original work.

APPENDIX E

Guidelines for Attentive Listening and Reflection*

*Adapted by JT Fest from a document by Donald Sharp

1. Listen patiently to what the other person has to say, even if you may believe it to be wrong or irrelevant. Indicate simple acceptance, not necessarily agreement, by nodding or using minimal encouragers (such as "mm-hmm" or "I see"). Remember that acknowledging is not condoning.

2. Do not get emotional. Simply try to understand first and defer evaluation.

3. Listen for the feelings behind the content. Many people, particularly young people, have difficulty expressing feelings clearly, making it important to pay close attention to the emotional context of what a person is saying.

4. Listen for what is *not* said. What a person chooses to leave out can be just as informative as what they choose to express.

5. Restate the person's feelings briefly, but as accurately as possible. "Mirror" the content while encouraging the other person to continue talking. Occasionally make summary responses such as "You think math is too hard," or "You feel the school is not meeting your needs." When doing so, keep your tone neutral and make a conscious effort to avoid "leading" the person to *your* conclusions.

6. When hearing a point that you wish to know more about, simply repeat the statement as a question. For example, you hear "Nobody cares about our ideas," you can probe by replying "Nobody cares about your ideas?" With this encouragement the previous statement will probably be expanded upon.

7. Avoid questioning or arguing about facts. Refrain from statements such as "Can you prove that," "That's not true," or "Wait a minute, let's look at what really happened." You may want to review facts later, but a review of facts has little to do with how a person feels right now.

8. If people get stuck and stop expressing themselves by saying "I don't know," you can often get them to think deeper by asking; "If you did know . . ." For example, a young person is trying to express what bothers them about a class. They get frustrated and say "Oh, I don't know." You then reply; "Well, if you did know what was bothering you, what might it be?"

9. If you are pressed with a genuine interest in your viewpoint, be honest in your reply. Try to be succinct, however, and quickly get back to the other person's views. In the listening stage, expression of your views may influence or inhibit what the other person says.

10. Most of all, BE QUIET. Let the other person talk. Attentively listening means taking a real *interest* in what the other person has to say.

APPENDIX F

Principles of Win/Win Negotiation for PYD Youth Work*
'Complied by JT Fest from various sources

Negotiation style comparison:

	WIN/LOSE	WIN/WIN
Focus:	• the position (what is wanted)	• the interest (why it is wanted)
Attitude:	• me versus you/us versus them	• us against the problem
Atmosphere:	• competition and mistrust	• collaboration and openness
Approaches:	• withholding information • deceit • threats • personal attacks	• disclosing information • honesty • encouragement • respect
Basis of Outcome:	• compromise • pressure • coercion • manipulation • prone to being sabotaged	• consensus • exploration • fairness • mutual interests and needs • likely to be upheld
Relationship:	• damaged or destroyed	• sustained or enhanced

Win/Win Negotiation Process:

1. Separate the people from the problem

- Consider each party's perception (for example by reversing roles)
- Make negotiation proposals consistent with the other party's interests
- Make emotions explicit and legitimate
- Use Attentive Listening

2. Focus on interests, not positions

- <u>Positions</u> may be thought of as one-dimensional points in a space of infinite possible solutions
- <u>Positions</u> are symbolic representations of a participant's underlying <u>interests</u>
- To discover <u>interests</u>, ask questions like:
  Why do you want this?
  What are you trying to satisfy?
  What would you like to accomplish?
  If you had what you are asking for, what would that look like or mean to you?
- In negotiation, there are *shared*, *compatible*, and *conflicting* <u>interests</u>
  It can be helpful to begin by identifying *shared* and *compatible* <u>interests</u> as "common ground" or "points of agreement" before working on *conflicting* interests. Principles can often be extrapolated from "points of agreement" to resolve other issues. Focusing on interests tends to direct the discussion to the *present* and *future*, and away from the *past*

3. Create Options for Mutual Gain

- Before seeking to reach agreement on solutions for the future, generate multiple options

  The typical way of doing this is through "brainstorming." In developing options, look for options that provide *mutual* gains.

4. Lighten It Up With Humor

- Negotiation should be FUN

  Look for ways to keep it light and playful

Phases of Negotiation: Try to be "(N)ICER."

Negotiation is
Initiation
Clarification
Exploration and
Resolution

Phase 1: Initiation

- Agree to set a positive, creative and supportive tone
- Create a comfortable environment (physical and psychological)
- Agree on ground rules -- listen to each other, treat each other with respect, agree on the amount of time you want to devote to the process, agree not to interrupt or express hostility or anger, and agree to listen to the other points of view
- Begin to separate the problem from the people

Phase 2: Clarification

- Agree generally on the purpose of the negotiations
- Outline and identify the problem
- Allow each person time to outline the issue and express his/her perspective
- Mutually clarify each other's understanding of the issues
- Mutually develop a list of topics for discussion

Phase 3: Exploration

- Explore underlying interests (needs, concerns, priorities)
- Discuss your own interests related to the particular issue at hand; express what is important and why
- Seek information from the other party regarding their interests and needs
- Identify mutual interests or areas of commonality
- Identify boundaries and limits
- Continue to encourage ongoing clarification and understanding of each other's point of view by listening, using open questions and paraphrasing
- Summarize both sets of interests related to the issues

Phase 4: <u>R</u>esolution

- Generate options for solutions together
- Avoid premature evaluation or the creativity will shut down
- Evaluate options against interests and agreed upon standards
- Develop strategies
- Discuss plans for implementation of a solution; who will do what, by when, and how?
- Be specific and concrete

Negotiation Do's and Don'ts:

<u>Do</u> . . .

- Pay attention
- Listen
- Show respect
- Take (all) concerns seriously
- Be aware of your assumptions and be willing to have them proved incorrect
- Pay attention to the balance of power

<u>Don't</u> . . .

- Treat it as competition or as a zero-sum game
- Forget that a negotiation is just one episode in an ongoing relationship

Most of all, **Don't** forget one fundamental rule:

Only one person can be angry at a time

Don't let situations escalate or you'll have a very hard time healing relationships and resolving issues.

FOOTNOTES:

Lesson 1: An Introduction to the Positive Youth Development Approach

1. Psychologists, researchers, and others have recognized human resilience for decades. It is usually described as the ability to withstand stress and trauma, and adapt to cope with setbacks and adversity. It doesn't mean that we don't experience or are not adversely affected by stress and trauma; only that we are able to work through it and even be strengthened by the experience. There is debate about whether resilience is something that we are born with, or whether it is a learned behavior, but there is no debate that all human beings have an innate capacity to demonstrate resilient behavior under the right conditions.

2. Werner, Emmy E., and Smith, Ruth S. (1992). *Overcoming the odds: High risk children from birth to adulthood.* Ithaca, NY: Cornell University Press.

3. Examples of Risk Factors include, but are not limited to, abuse/neglect, family conflict, poor family support, substance use/abuse, poor or unstable housing or homelessness, extreme economic or social deprivation, community deterioration or disorganization, community violence and/or gangs, inadequate education and recreational opportunities, mental or physical health issues, learning disabilities, early unplanned pregnancy, and cultural and/or linguistic isolation.

4. Like many aspects of PYD, Protective Factors are sometimes presented in different manners or numbers depending on the source. This presentation represents a consensus view.

Lesson 2: Youth Outcomes: The "Bottom Line" of Youth Work

5. The Advancing Youth Development curriculum was created by the Academy for Educational Development/Center for Youth Development and Policy Research, in collaboration with the National Network for Youth, which was the product of a 3-year project funded by the Office of Juvenile Justice and Delinquency Prevention (OJJDP) at the U.S. Department of Justice. The Academy for Educational Development effectively ceased to exist when it combined with Family Health International to create FHI 360.

6. Positive Youth Development in the United States: Research Findings on Evaluations of Positive Youth Development Programs, by Richard F. Catalano, Ph.D.; M. Lisa Berglund, Ph.D.; Jeanne A.M. Ryan, M.S.C.I.S.; Heather S. Lonczak, M.A.; J. David Hawkins, Ph.D.; Social Development Research Group, University of Washington School of Social Work, Seattle, Washington, November 13, 1998. Funded by and submitted to: U.S. Department of Health and Human Services, Office of the Assistant Secretary for Planning and Evaluation, and National Institute for Child Health and Human Development.

Lesson 3: (s)OS: A Framework for Youth Development

7. Maslow, A.H. A theory of human motivation. Psychological Review, July 1943

Lesson 4: High Expectations

8. It doesn't matter whether you pick the red or black Joker ... your choice.
9. Los Angeles Times, March 13, 2004, "City Officials Fall for Internet Hoax."
10. The concept of Fight or Flight can be traced to Walter Cannon in 1929 [Cannon WB: Bodily Changes in Pain, Hunger, Fear and Rage: An Account of Recent Research Into the Function of Emotional Excitement, 2nd ed. New York, Appleton-Century-Crofts, 1929]. Since that time there have been several variations on the theory. In the article "Does 'Fight or Flight' need updating" [Bracha, Dr. Stefan and Williams, Andrew E. and Bracha, Adam S., 2004], the authors suggest that a "Freeze" response precedes any fight or flight, and that the proper way to phrase our reaction to fear should be a "Freeze, _Flight_ or Fight," as they contend that we will freeze first, and then attempt flight behavior before fight behavior. I don't think conceding a freeze response in any way changes the validity of the discussion in this lesson. Whether or not there are things that come before fight or flight only gives us additional clues to avoid escalating the perceived threat. But it does make a difference if we believe that we will attempt flight before fight, or even if we believe that fight or flight is the true order. Personally, I don't think there is a hard and fast order. I believe that "fight or flight" are two options we consider based on our assessment of their effectiveness in any given situation. Perhaps all things being equal, we will flee before we fight -- but all things are never equal. A frightened street-dependent youth may always resort to fight behavior before flight behavior based on his/her experience that tells them that fight is the most effective way

to eliminate the threat. Regardless of these factors, both fight and flight behaviors indicate a youth who is fearful, and the most effective response is to address issues of safety.

11. *Pygmalion in the classroom: teacher expectation and pupils' intellectual development.* New York: Holt, Rinehart and Winston, 1968.

Lesson 5: Meaningful Participation

12. See Strategies of Participation later in this lesson.
13. More information on the adolescent concept of time is contained in Street Culture 2.0: An epistemology of Street-dependent Youth, available at http://www.in4y.com
14. Compilation prepared by JT Fest based on Strategies for Youth Participation by Gill Westhorp of the Youth Sector Training Council, Australia; the Foundation for Young Australians; Advancing Youth Development by the AED/Center for Youth Development and Policy Research in collaboration with the National Network for Youth, Inc.; and original work.
15. "Ad Hoc" is used here to mean that the input is improvised or impromptu; more of an "on the spot" form of input rather than a planned or structured form.

Lesson 6: Caring, Supportive Relationships

16. Interestingly, this matches the "7 +/- 2" concept described in Street Culture 2.0: An epistemology of Street-dependent Youth, available at http://www.in4y.com
17. Often referred to as "Active" Listening, I prefer the term "Attentive" Listening. "Active," to me, puts the emphasis on the actions you take to apply listening skills. On the other hand, "Attentive" puts the emphasis on the attention you are giving to what is being said. It underscores that it is more important to *hear* than it is to *listen.*
18. The concept of "self-government" in youth programs was an idea that I adapted from A.S. Neill's work at Summerhill School, and applied to several residential settings for street-dependent youth. "Self-government" means that youth are self-regulating and hold themselves accountable to guidelines and structures that they have a role in creating.

Bonus Lesson: Measuring Developmental Outcomes

19. 2013 figures.
20. Primarily Safety and Structure, Physical/Mental Health, and Intellectual Ability, though these promises touch on all developmental needs.

Appendix D: A Spectrum of Youth Participation -- An Evolutionary View

21. "Time Commitment" refers to the time adult staff will need to dedicate to support activities.

ABOUT THE AUTHOR

JT (Jerry) Fest is a youth advocate, consultant and trainer specializing in the Positive Youth Development approach, Trauma-informed Care, issues of homelessness and programs for youth with specific expertise in programs for runaway and homeless youth. He founded and was the Program Director of Janus Youth Program's Willamette Bridge; a continuum of programs including streetwork/outreach (Yellow Brick Road of Portland), emergency shelter (Street Light Youth Shelter), transitional living (Bridge House), independent living & case management (Changes), and youth business and partnership programs. In 1987 he developed the "self-government" model for residential services at the Bridge House program; one of the earliest program designs based on the principles of Positive Youth Development.

Mr. Fest has served on the Board of Directors of the Northwest Network for Youth, the National Network for Youth, and served two terms as the Region Ten representative to the National Council for Youth Policy representing federally funded runaway and homeless youth programs in Alaska, Idaho, Oregon and Washington State. He is experienced as a federal Peer Monitor and Peer Monitor trainer for the U.S. Department of Health and Human Services, Administration for Children and Families, and as an Expert Witness for cases involving street-dependent/homeless youth and adults. He is the recipient of the 1996 Oregon Child and Youth Care Association "Citizen of the Year" award for his work with street-dependent (homeless) youth, and the Year 2000 Helen Reser Bakkensen award for *exemplary leadership, service, and advocacy on behalf of homeless youth.*

In 1999 Mr. Fest left Willamette Bridge to become a full-time consultant and trainer on the national level, where he developed the "Winning Hand" presentation upon which this workbook is based. His clients have included the Administration for Children and Families, Head Start, Job Corps, public and private schools, and a diverse community of private non-profit organizations.

Made in the USA
Middletown, DE
21 September 2018